Feeding the Hustle

Feeding the Hustle

Free Food & Care
Inside the Tech Industry

Jesse Dart

LEXINGTON BOOKS
Lanham • Boulder • New York • London

Published by Lexington Books
An imprint of The Rowman & Littlefield Publishing Group, Inc.
4501 Forbes Boulevard, Suite 200, Lanham, Maryland 20706
www.rowman.com

86-90 Paul Street, London EC2A 4NE

British Library Cataloguing in Publication Information Available

Library of Congress Cataloging-in-Publication Data

Names: Dart, Jesse, author.
Title: Feeding the hustle : free food & care inside the tech industry / Jesse Dart.
Description: Lanham : Lexington Books, [2022] | Includes bibliographical references and index.
Identifiers: LCCN 2021048373 (print) | LCCN 2021048374 (ebook) | ISBN 9781793635013 (cloth ; alk. paper) | ISBN 9781793635020 (ebook)
Subjects: LCSH: Employee fringe benefits. | Corporate culture. | Organizational behavior. | Industrial relations. | Internet industry—Personnel management.
Classification: LCC HD4928.N6 D37 2022 (print) | LCC HD4928.N6 (ebook) | DDC 331.25/5—dc23
LC record available at https://lccn.loc.gov/2021048373
LC ebook record available at https://lccn.loc.gov/2021048374

♾️™ The paper used in this publication meets the minimum requirements of American National Standard for Information Sciences—Permanence of Paper for Printed Library Materials, ANSI/NISO Z39.48-1992.

Contents

Preface

In November of 1999, Charlie Ayers was the fifty-third employee to be hired at Google, then a small startup company. Charlie wasn't an engineer, a programmer, a marketing wiz, or even a salesperson. He was a chef.

Food has always been closely linked to the office as well as anthropological studies. A packed lunch, a working lunch, lunch at your desk, no lunch, and so on, these ideas of eating are all part of the food culture of the workplace, along with so many variations it's impossible to list them all. But by hiring Charlie, Google put food front and center for its employees and their workplace philosophy, and perhaps the tech office has never been the same since.

This is arguably the beginning of what I believe are extreme office perks—free meals, unlimited snacks and drinks, on-site doctors and oil changes, the list goes on and on. It's easy to see how attractive this must have been to potential employees. Never before had a new hire been able to access what was essentially a demystified executive dining room—in fact, Google essentially killed the executive dining room by opening it up to all employees. The executive dining room used to be one of the benefits of a long career and promotion along with the corner office. It was something to look forward to. While this idea was popular and probably most resilient in the world of finance, the tech industry began their push toward openness starting with the cafeteria. This idea spread like wildfire and soon, more and more companies, not just tech companies, were offering employees snacks, drinks, and complete meals, all for free.

Accordingly, food occupies a prominent role in the anthropology I want to develop here.

Lunch has become functional instead of social. This is how one tech worker explained his lunch break to me after starting to work from home during the

COVID-19 pandemic. He took less time to eat lunch than he did in the office and misses the relief he used to feel from not having to worry or think about what to prepare. What he expressed is, I believe, an overall aching for the social aspects of eating, a feeling that most, if not all of us can identify with. Considering his company's situation, he told a story from early on in the pandemic about receiving a message from an executive stating that free food and snacks are a perk, and while working from home, those are not perks that can be expensed. Free meals have limits; free meals are "office-bound" ideas of care and control.

The research for this book was conducted before the COVID-19 pandemic began. That being said, none of the offices I was in are currently operating in the same way. Moreover, all the food program managers that I interviewed no longer have their jobs. Not only has the pandemic changed the physical space in which tech workers perform their jobs and are served free meals, but it has also had wide ranging side effects on several other support industries, namely, those that employ workers who cook and clean in these offices.

While my research uncovers anthropological ideas about value and care, it also, in light of the pandemic, shows that the kinds of workplace scenarios that most tech workers were part of were unnecessary. From the free food to the office space, neither is now seen as essential. On top of this, the idea of overwork, while being supported by free meals, snacks, and drinks, has not been undone because workers have to buy their own. Instead, it's thrived, showing that the cult of overwork is not related to space, but to the ways in which employees consider their jobs, pressure to impress and succeed, and the nature of knowledge work itself. Just because we start working from home doesn't mean these pressures and work ethics are diminished.

Anyone reading the news about the changing nature of work this past year will have noticed that tech companies were ahead of the game about allowing employees to work from home, while in the past these same companies have championed the ways in which being in the office helps creativity. While those results are yet to come in, what these companies have seen is a massive increase in stock valuation and profit. Their bottom line hasn't been disparaged by the shift to work-from-home but has benefited from the difficult global circumstances.

Other implications of the pandemic include what has been deemed an exodus of people leaving the San Francisco Bay Area and moving to cheaper locales. Texas and Arizona are popular, as are Florida and Georgia. Working from home has become one way of keeping a relatively high salary, while making that money go further. Some states like Texas already have established tech industries, and an added incentive is that it has no state income taxes, a policy that makes living there with even a low six-figure salary enticing. Where individuals and families once could only afford apartments or rentals, many find once they leave the Bay Area houses are more affordable and their quality of life remains the same or increases. Gone are the pee-soaked streets, the needles, the homeless people everywhere, part of life in San Francisco that most employees who lived or worked there got used to, along with $6 coffees and $15 burritos.

It is interesting to note that employees are getting more used to the fact that their lunches and snacks will no longer be provided for free in the office, or that they will never go back to the office. So, what does care of these employees look like now, while working from home? How does a company compensate for these perks in other ways (or not) and what happens to all the workers whose jobs were to prepare and feed employees? These are questions for a future research project. It's early, and too soon to see how the pandemic will continue to shape the nature of work in the tech industry. But it's not too soon to see that the impact it has had, has not been completely negative. Not at all.

Author's note: The names of people and companies in this book are pseudonyms and have been changed from their original.

Introduction

When they told me that I got free lunch and all the snacks, I took the job immediately.

—Katie, employee, Company B, London

On a sunny day in May 2017, I went to meet a colleague for a coffee at a cafe near Mint Plaza in the Financial District of San Francisco, an urban jungle of cement and steel near the eastern part of the city. The skyscrapers that rose into the famous fog made me wonder about the effects of earthquakes. The streets were as you would find in many cities, filled with chain cafes and stores—down the center of many were tram rails, and overhead ran electric wires for the busses. That part of town bordered "The Tenderloin." Local lore says it was named that because of the tendency for restaurants in the area to serve free fried tenderloin sandwiches to the police in order to persuade them to patrol the area. Now, it seems, the smell of fried tenderloin has been replaced with the smell of urine.

I hadn't been in town for long, having arrived just a few days before, and this was my first time in the heart of the city. Exiting the BART train at Powell Street, I got turned around walking to the cafe and meandered down Sixth Street. Along my path, a couple of people were passed out near a bus stop, one man was on the ground with his pants pulled down to his knees next to an angry woman with a shopping cart yelling, and, again, there was a harsh smell of urine. It was 4 p.m. on a Thursday afternoon. Given the way most people just went along with their business, it seemed this was not out of the ordinary. This is San Francisco, I thought, and this is the scene in the middle of all this wealth? There were people in suits and fancy shoes—just around the corner were fine dining restaurants. What was going on?

I arrived at the cafe to meet my friend, Pamela. "You look a bit out of it. Are you okay?" she asked. I told her the path I took, down Sixth Street. Her eyes grew big, and she shook her head—"Oh man, I'm sorry, I should have warned you." Our conversation continued over coffee that felt too expensive and we came back around to my naive view of the city. I had done my research, I had read just about everything I could get my hands on about the disparity in the city, I already knew there was a gap between the haves and have-nots, and I started referring to it as "tech vs. the rest." Pam agreed, "You're right, and it's getting worse. Even in the East Bay, you have many of the same issues."

I just couldn't get past the fact that there was a stench of stale yellow pee that pervaded the downtown area of this major city. In a sense, it was a very sensorial introduction to the problems that the city faces. It's become such an issue that in 2018, the City of San Francisco created a street-cleaning task group—not just to combat urine, but human feces on the sidewalks.

San Francisco was once the counterculture capital. Today, the counterculture still exists on the margins of a city that is quickly becoming a greater symbol for the division between rich and poor. Anyone looking for the summer of love and the free rein of the 1960s and early 1970s will find nothing of the like. It is now the second most expensive city in America, after New York. Rents for a studio apartment are near $4000 a month and Golden Gate Park, where most of the "Summer of Love" took place, is no longer safe at night for those walking through it. The tech industry has greatly inflated the cost of living in the city. Highly paid workers have flooded the Bay Area and rents have shot up. Newspaper headlines read, "Scraping by on Six Figures? Tech Workers Feel Poor in Silicon Valley's Wealth Bubble" (Solon 2017) and "Ordinary People Can't Afford a Home in San Francisco. How Did It Come to This?" (La Ganga 2016).

The smell of latrine is one that has been noted in many journalistic articles about the city. Thomas Fuller, writing in the *New York Times*, states that life on the dirtiest street in San Francisco includes regular occurrences like stepping over needles and human feces (Fuller 2018). But passing urine-soaked streets and a sizeable homeless population seems par for the course for many of the tech employees working in downtown San Francisco. It was a startling realization and introduction to the city.

NO SUCH THING AS A FREE LUNCH?

Meanwhile, inside the towering glass and steel structures were beautiful displays of fruit, sushi, pizza, burgers, snacks, and a wall of drinks—all for free, removed from the pee-scented streets below. On my first day at Company A in San Francisco, it was impossible, at least for me, to walk inside and not be surprised at the amount and variety of food that was available for employees. During my fieldwork I found myself taking granola bars or a drink away with me at the end of the day: it felt like I had given in to a temptation.

A culture of free food has developed in the tech industry over the past fifteen years in which the objective is to increase productivity (which is difficult to measure and define), attract and retain employees, and create a sense of community by dining together. What you find, once inside these offices, is an open floor plan with rows of desks, busy employees on their company-supplied Apple laptops, and a system of feeding people that is reminiscent of what James Watson says could be 1950s China—where food relieves employees from everyday domestic chores in order to have more time to devote to work (Watson 2010, 386). This is the hustle; giving in to the corporate idea of working more, working longer, but with the added perks of not having to do anything else.

Free food programs have become nearly compulsory within the tech industry. No tech company wants to be the odd one out.[1] While some companies offer subsidized food instead of free food (like Apple and Microsoft) this research is focused entirely on two companies with exclusively free food for employees, which here I call Company A and Company B. My investigation is mostly concerned with the experiences of employees as opposed to the pure economics of the programs. When someone decides to purchase a product, even if at reduced cost, it triggers a level of social awareness and consideration. Free food, on the other hand, can be attained mindlessly. Grazing can happen every time an employee passes by the kitchen area and often does. My research is not about demonizing tech companies or their food programs. Nor is it about the nutritional aspects of what is served and eaten. Instead, it is about the social relations around food in tech offices and how food and commensality are ways to divide and to unite.

The main research question is how do we understand commensality in the workplace? Some hold it as a way to build teamwork and cooperation. Others imply it is a kind of nefarious corporate plot to get workers to stay at the office longer. In approaching this question, I'll traverse related questions, such as: how is eating so many meals together at work changing workplace relationships and dynamics? If you control the food, do you control the employee? And, is eating in the workplace linked someway to job satisfaction and happiness?

There are two main concepts that emerged during my fieldwork that help to answer these questions—gifting and commensality. While these represent the core of the anthropology that I want to develop, the concepts of care and precarity help to place them within the tech industry and the offices I spent time in.

Commensality is fairly straightforward: at its basic level, it simply means eating with other people, at the same table (Fischler 2011). Within the tech industry commensality can be seen through the idea of insider/outsider eating: for instance, in San Francisco this is played out with the homeless on the streets below excluded from the free food in the offices. This is a case of literally "in-group sharing" of food. Commensality is about belonging but also about exclusion. The ability of shared food to unite but also divide is a recurring theme.

I'll use James Carrier's definition of the gift to help make sense of the kinds of social bond and exchanges taking place in these offices. He says a gift is

> a thing given from one person to another as part of an enduring social relationship. The thing given may be a physical object but may be immaterial, for example, labor, names, titles, or hospitality. The giver may but need not be an individual: a house-hold, a lineage, or a group of neighbors can give. In linking gifts to social relationships, this view differs from the individualist view that links them only to the sentiments of the giver. (Carrier 2018, 1)

Gift exchange logics are oftentimes based on emotion and feeling—the passions provoked by gifts (or their absence) can be weird, subjective, and unstable. Mauss's discussion of the gift has inspired anthropological research on the subject over the decades, from a number of different perspectives and locations. This is, as Carrier tells us, in part because "the Gift is about a fundamental process: people's dealings with each other in social relationships and especially transactions with each other" (Carrier 2018). What I found is that the idea that free food is a gift (in these offices) really depends on whom you ask. This is where the weird emotional logics that govern gift exchange come into play. For example, how do individuals know how much work to do in exchange for free food? Why do some people feel guilty for taking a lot of snacks and others don't? How much food is enough? I found that these were questions that circulated around free food programs with no clear-cut answers.

Finally, it is important not to overlook the larger social issues of precarious labor and unstable futures supported by a peculiar, often superficial, kind of care. To that point, Benson and Kirsch tell us that anthropological critiques of the corporation cannot avoid engaging with larger social and environmental problems, including the "corrosive problems of inequality and the threat of global climate change, which suggest the need for structural changes to the economy and improved governance of transnational corporations" (Benson and Kirsch 2018, 7).

The kinds of care that I witnessed in these offices raise the question of whether or not this is true care because those who are actually providing it (i.e., office managers or similar, catering companies, chefs) are being paid to do so, which in turn makes one believe that their care is just another type of labor—just another job in an office (Lane 2017, 4). It brings to mind ideas about the nature of care itself in the context of an office—where it might be expected that those who are responsible for providing it be more invested in the employees than they are in the money they receive. The food program managers I spoke to didn't enjoy the same financial remuneration as many of those employees they were caring for. This in turn left some of them unengaged, unempathetic, and uninterested. With this in mind, we also must turn to the idea of what food is being offered. Is it meant to be enticing, to make the jobs more attractive or seem more fun? Or instead is it meant to be physically nourishing, which implies a level of care for the physical well-being of the workers? There are both ideas at play in these offices, as we'll see later on.

Studying Sideways

My research brings into question the concept of doing ethnographic research at home. The fieldwork that forms the backbone of this book was completed over the course of thirteen months spent between San Francisco (in my home country of the United States) and London (where I had been living for the five years previous) inside the offices of Company A and Company B (more on them below). So, on the one hand, this research raises the question: how can anthropologists be immersed in the field when it is in many respects familiar? On the other hand, tech companies' food programs factor in, I will show, elements of "homeyness" in the office, including maternal office managers and cleaners, and an emphasis on personal touches. This raises a second question: can organizations become "homes" for the people who work there, or indeed for the ethnographers who study them?

During my time in the field, I felt at home in the cities I lived in but felt like an outsider in the organizations I studied. Attempting to appreciate my own understanding of these situations brought me again and again back to a set of questions inspired by Aldo Merlino's auto-ethnographic research into driving habits in Argentina, his home country (Merlino 2015, 10):

- Why am I really interested in the topic of tech offices?
- What feelings did or do I have about offices and workspaces?
- Have I been positioning myself as a researcher over those who work in this industry?
- What allowed me to think that my findings could be of some use to society?

Questions like these unsettle the taken-for-granted comforts of doing field-work at home and also provided a lodestar in the sometimes-disorientating swamp of the familiar. At the same time, these questions encouraged me to utilize the ethnographer (me!) as a kind of informant. These questions have helped me along in the discipline of understanding the landscape of the tech offices and my relationship with them. Akin to Merlino (2015), Fox (2004), and Feliu (2007), I have tried to leave the "made by anyone, from anywhere" style of writing behind. I have adopted instead "a style of writing in which the researcher is involved and responsible for the processes described" (Merlino 2015, 9). In the following chapters, I endeavor to interlace my own insights, field notes, and conversations into the ethnography not only as a way of un-derstanding the processes I witnessed and was involved in but also as a way of engaging the reader in an academic and empathetic way (Given 2008).

I am inspired by anthropologists who "study up," such as Laura Nader, Susan Ostrander, Karen Ho, and Sherry Ortner. The connection between their work and my own is a focus on "upper-class elites." I set out with this in mind, but was surprised when I realized that in fact, what I was doing was studying, as Ortner says, sideways—as many of the employees I interviewed and worked with would be considered solidly middle class.[2] Ortner takes this into account when she says, "Studying up is really 'studying sideways,' that is, studying people—like scientists, journalists, and Hollywood filmmak-ers—who in many ways are really not much different from anthropologists and our fellow academics more generally" (Ortner 2010, 213). She was most likely drawing on Hannerz, and his interpretation of where anthropological research is headed. He says:

> But then as some anthropologists focused their ethnographic curiosity on people with practices not so unlike their own, this could really be labeled as "studying sideways." . . . Recently, moreover, the field has sometimes been "here and there," in many sites, trans- or multi- something or other. (Hannerz 2006, 24)

One of the reasons why many social scientists are wary of studying up, according to Ostrander, is the perceived difficulty of gaining access and building rapport (Ostrander 1993). Ostrander's examples of gaining access to different elite groups and companies in the early 1990s were not that dif-ferent from my own issues in gaining access to my field sites. The methods of communication might be different (emails instead of faxes and phone calls) but, like her, I started at the top and worked my way down, utilizing every contact, friend of a friend, and connection I could possibly think of.

In "Up the Anthropologist" Laura Nader urges anthropologists to "engage in the critical study of dominant institutions" and what she calls the "control-ling processes" in countries like the United States (Nader 1972, 289). I can think of no more dominant institution in the United States (nay, the world) than the tech industry. Thinking back to Maria, the Polish girl at Company A in London, I wonder whether she is an elite above me? The idea of the elite tech worker is very much based on an idea of this kind of employee in California. In London, the tech industry is still minor compared to the combined industries that circle around finance. The salaries that employees make in satellite offices of companies like Company B and Company A don't put them in the same position as those in the financial services industry. Google and Facebook are perhaps the only companies with salaries that approach those levels (according to reported salaries on Glassdoor.com). To some extent, this extends to the variations in food in each office too. In San Francisco, the food presented something that many people outside the industry might consider elitist: organic, healthy, clean, personalized, and so on. In satellite offices, the food was, for lack of a better word, humbler—less "California Cuisine," more reheated buffet.

Nader addresses the problem of access in her writing, paraphrasing the objections based on access: "The powerful are out of reach on a number of different planes, they don't want to be studied, it is dangerous to study the powerful, they are busy people, they are not all in one place, etc." (Nader 1972, 302). The challenges are true for anthropologists in many places, and we face "problems of access" everywhere. Solving these problems is what constitutes building rapport, in her opinion, and is a very integral part of the fieldwork process. You can learn a lot about the companies or community of people you want to study through the process of gaining access. Finally, Nader spells it out for us, that it's surprising that we should be timid of doing research at home than in some dangerous and even hostile environments that anthropologists seem so drawn to:

> If we look at the literature based on field work in the United States, we find a relatively abundant literature on the poor, the ethnic groups, the disadvantaged; there is comparatively little field research on the middle class and very little first-hand work on the upper classes. Anthropologists might indeed ask themselves whether the entirety of fieldwork does not depend upon a certain power relationship in favor of the anthropologist and whether indeed such dominant-subordinate relationships may not be affecting the kinds of theories we are weaving. What if, in reinventing anthropology, anthropologists were to study the colonizers rather than the colonized, the culture of power rather than the culture of the powerless, the culture of affluence rather than the culture of poverty? (Nader 1972, 289)

Anthropologists have always had to be adaptable in their methods according to their object of study. While all anthropologists are aware of the mythologized image of the rugged and solo ethnographer setting out to do fieldwork on some tropical beach as laid down by Malinowski in *Argonauts of the Western Pacific*, the reality is that the discipline has always been more diverse than this.

Food is an excellent vehicle for addressing what we might call polymorphous ethnography, or the more "radical" term, multi-sited ethnography. Many anthropologists working in the anthropology of food have been grappling with this type of research for some time. From following food chains (Belasco and Horowitz 2009) to understanding food in schools (Salazar 2007, Andersen et al. 2015) to investigations on production methods (Jennings et al. 2005, Foster and Palgrave 2008), multi-sited work has helped facilitate these types of inquiries. Or, as George Marcus mentions, multi-sited ethnography's goal is not a holistic representation and "ethnographic portrayal of the world system as a totality" (Marcus 1995, 99).

The Cartography of Feeding the Hustle

Constructing an ethnography of tech offices and their free food programs in different cities and countries is showcased in each chapter—tying together ideas of commensality and gifting and relating back to the research question across eight chapters. When read separately, each provides a glimpse into one aspect of these spaces. But when read together, they provide a larger picture of what is happening inside these offices. The chapters reflect the different spaces and together convey what, from the outside, might seem perfectly normal or simple. What I show is how strange they actually are. These food spaces not only enact a kind of gifting culture, but also function as a substitute home. I start out with that concept and use other examples from anthropological literature to show that the idea of home is socially constructed, shifting, difficult to pin down, and personal.

Chapter 2 takes aim at the theory of studying sideways and studying up, and it's here that I begin to construct what life is like for me, the temporary tech-worker/non-worker and my own introduction into what the workday consists of. Coffee machine chats and beginning to understand that I am part of this group in one way or another are discussed.

The idea of home usually goes together with family. Dining together as a group (commensality) is an important social phenomenon and I wanted to get to the heart of that in the workplace. Chapter 3 lays the groundwork for feeding employees through a look at the significance of the family meal in restaurants. With examples from the field, this chapter solidifies the point that eating together is a significant part of team building, collaboration, and creating a sense of belonging (all concepts that are very important to tech companies). But the restaurants I visited would never think of not feeding their employees. Yet, the programs of free food in the tech industry can be fleeting.

In chapter 4, I discuss the fact that free food is not promised and can be (and was) cut from companies' budgets—food programs generate zero income for the companies and are some of the first things to get cut when finances are tight. To make my point, I talk about the importance of snacks, the fascination with and importance of LaCroix sparkling water, and coffee and caffeinated spaces and discuss the how the financial health of the company can be viewed through food programs. In the end, gifts like these have a financial cost and can turn into tools that actually encourage the growth of a culture of entitlement that some people (especially managers!) found irritating, ungracious, and an overall negative effect of the food program.

An important lesson learned during my fieldwork was the significance of space in the office and how space can impact the food programs in unforeseen ways. Chapter 5 focuses on space and place. Here I consider the open office, the importance of unused kitchen spaces, and how Company B's offices represented a considered use of space for their employees and food program. Commensality has much to do with where you eat (as much as with whom). This leads into chapter 6, where I take a new look at commensality, institutional dining, and productivity in these offices. Starting off with a consideration of the concepts of commensal units and commensal circles to show the relevance of workplace commensality, I follow up with some real-world examples of commensality taken from social media.

In chapter 7, I take a worker's view of the tech industry and discuss how labor practices are interrelated to the food programs, benefits, and perks these companies offer. I use examples from the field and utilize other ethnographic work, such as Karen Ho's account from the financial industry to support the idea that in many tech companies, taking a full lunch break is a sign of not pitching in enough and that these programs support the hustle culture. I show that commensality is linked to the nature of work in this industry and draw on the labor theories of David Harvey to understand how labor has shifted from a "Fordist" model to a more flexible way of working.

Finally, in chapter 8, I write a conclusion that captures the tone and breadth of the study, one that understands that there is so much more to discover and understand in these unique spaces, but also I reflect on what the limits of care are in these offices—and how care can be neglected, taken away, and restored.

Each chapter includes ethnographic accounts in the form of field notes and observations accumulated over the course of the research, transcripts of conversations, and photographs from the field (especially of the many meals

I ate), which I hope help to place you inside these companies' workspaces. I conducted approximately fifty semi-structured interviews, focused on themes and ideas of free food in an office, and approximately twenty-five more informal interviews outside of the office with not just workers in the tech industry, but those in restaurants (another example of an industry that usually provides a meal for employees). Semi-structured interviews were recorded, transcribed, and coded for themes. Informal interviews held outside of the office in pubs, cafes, bars, and parks and on the street provided rich, textual content in the form of field notes. I incorporate a wide use of images in my work, took countless audio recordings of office noises, and recorded sensorial aspects of the spaces including temperature, smell, and noise. These all contribute to "being there" and developing an in-depth understanding of what it means to work in these spaces.

Many of the meals may look similar and there was a theme that emerged: there were lots of salads, lasagna was popular, burgers were not served as often as I had anticipated, there was an overabundance of proteins (oftentimes mixed), and chicken is still one of the most consumed things anywhere. The meals I ate not only contributed to my own ability to work but also provided a nice place for casual exchanges and interactions in each office. I found that the lunch table was a space where employees were willing to talk about a number of topics, share common experiences, and learn about each other. Over many meals I made new friends and became integrated into the offices I spent time in and discovered that these spaces are a perfect place to conduct research full of anthropological ideas that we normally might not consider. With that in mind, I pulled up a chair and dug in.

NOTES

1. This was pre COVID-19.
2. See Solon (2017).

A new report from the Department of Housing and Urban Development from June 2018 says that a San Francisco metro area family of four bringing in $117,400 a year qualifies as "low income," In 2017 the cutoff was $105,350. An annual salary of $82,000 now puts single adults in the "low income" bracket as well (http://www.cnbc.com/2018/06/28/families-earning-117000-qualify-as-low-income-in-san-francisco.html).

Chapter One

On How to Do Fieldwork in a Tech Office

I first became interested in studying free food in the tech industry after reading an article about all the benefits these employees received that those of us who don't work for a tech company might lust after. It was blatantly obvious that the piece was trying to prove how much other companies don't care about their employees because they didn't offer unlimited free food, snacks, drinks, coffee, and beer. No free on-site gym, no desk massages once a week.

My first thought was of high school and how parochial this appeared. The second was that I didn't enjoy eating with my colleagues, and usually ate alone—why would I want to spend more time with the people I already spend so much time with, possibly even more time than with my wife? It seemed like an insane idea at the time. At this point, it had been a while since I had lived in the United States, so my perception of American workplace culture might have been skewed by my time spent working in offices in London.

My path toward studying the culture of free food at work started with a connection to the food program director at Google. Each and every employee at Google has access to free food and it's this unique fact that really gave me the itch to know more. In his book *Work Rules! Insights from Inside Google That Will Transform How You Live and Lead,* Laszlo Bock, Google's VP of people, mentions the benefits of food for employees. To this end, he references a letter from the founders from their 2004 IPO offering where they explain their "unusual benefits" including free meals and doctors and washing machines, and continue by saying that they intend to "add benefits over time" and that benefits can "save employees considerable time and improve their health and productivity" (Bock 2015, 260).

With their benefits package, Google set a standard which almost every other tech company has, to some degree, imitated, and also reinforces the importance of health in the workplace. Free food is just one step toward a new revolutionary, transformative force in the corporate world. While statistics about how many tech companies provide free food are difficult to come by, it is safe to say that more often than not there is some kind of food being provided. That might be simply free tea and coffee, snacks, fruit, or full meals.

Knowing that Google was such a large company, I realized that I needed to find slightly smaller versions. The two companies I conducted long-term research at I will call "Company A" and "Company B." While not the largest companies operating in the tech industry, they do have a significant global presence. I spent countless hours emailing, calling, and Skyping a number of tech companies to try and gain access over the course of a year. It was tricky. For every company whose food program manager said yes, their lawyers said no. This initially made me wonder why. Were they perhaps scared about what I would find? Maybe, but it most likely had more to do with intellectual property than it did the food programs. I finally hit upon two companies that were very open to the project. After the initial emails to the "gatekeepers," being the EMEA (European, Middle East Area) director of Company A in London and the global food program manager at Company B in New York, and a few non-disclosure forms later, I entered the field.[1, 2]

It should be said here that I am talking about a specific kind of tech company, of which there are several. I am referring to companies that commodify user-produced objects and data through an internet-based software application. This is not the entire world of tech companies, and in fact, the use of the single phrase "tech companies" conflates hardware, software, internet-based, and mobile app companies. Company A was established in 2006 and Company B in 2005 and neither is considered to be a startup or a more established Silicon Valley company. This isn't to say that there is a considerable amount of crossover in the kinds of jobs that exist in each kind of company, only that the business model differs.

When I started my research at Company A's London office there were thirty-five employees. There, I was able to interview about twenty employees one-on-one. Informally, though, at lunch, at the cafe around the corner, or at the pub, I spoke and interacted with others.

Next, I moved over to Company B's London office, with a similar number of employees: around thirty. There, one-on-one interviews were harder to arrange, and I managed about fifteen. I also gathered useful data from joining the communal lunch table and casual chats around the coffee machines.

In San Francisco, Company A's office held around three hundred employees. Challenges in arranging formal interviews included the constantly booked meeting rooms (and my inability to access the online booking platform) and a general air of "busyness" that permeated the office. What this site lacked in formal interviews (I conducted fifteen), it made up for in informal interviews and observation. In this office, everyone assumed I was just another new employee—I blended in, and this was an advantage.

Down the street at Company B's San Francisco office, I interviewed over half of the office of thirty. They were a talkative group, both formally and informally, and it's here that I logged some of the longest conversations, a few pushing over a couple of hours long. I finished up my fieldwork with a short but meaningful stay in Dublin, where Company B once again opened their doors to me. It was the most beautiful office I worked in, and the employees were equally as open and ready to talk. In Dublin I conducted five interviews.

Spaced throughout my fieldwork were interviews with chefs, restaurant workers, startup companies who deal with office food, lunches at Google in London and Sydney, informal chats with Twitter employees, and a host of informal conversations with friends, family, and colleagues, all of whom seemed to have a story or opinion or knew someone working in a tech office with these "crazy" benefits. In restaurants, I tried to understand the concept of care of employees through researching the family meal. At Google, I had tantalizing opportunities to occasionally sample what I believe was the apex of free food for workers and had the opportunity to interview a number of its employees.

Just a few months into the fieldwork, I attended a conference in London on how to care for employees, called "Employee Benefits Live," which was billed as "Europe's largest dedicated reward & benefits event for the HR industry."[3] Some of the topics and seminars included "best practices in integrating people and technology to create a culture of increased health and well-being" and "engaging multi-generational workplaces." While this conference was focused on benefits for mostly non-technology related companies, it was fascinating as a researcher to understand the ways in which employee wellness and perks were packaged and "sold" to companies by other companies.

I ate countless meals inside the offices, drank a lot of coffee, went to the corner pub on Fridays for an after-work pint with employees (in the UK offices, that is). I took public transport to the office, and I was assigned desk space in every office (and even a locker for my things at Company A in San Francisco). I felt like an employee and to some extent, I was one. Employees let me into their offices, their lives, and their world. I asked them about their work, their lives, and the free food, meals, snacks, drinks, and perks in their offices to find out more about how this way of being in a tech office is affecting the social aspects of this particular group of people. I also learned to play Ping-Pong during my fieldwork. These tables seemed to be in every tech office as a clear statement to anyone inside that you were in fact in a tech office. The Ping-Pong table[4] is the cultural artifact of the tech office—it is the ultimate statement of leisure, play, and freedom.

Most of the offices I visited felt sterile—clean and bright, but not warm or welcoming. This goes against what I had perceived before starting my field-work to be an important part of these spaces: that they begin to feel like home. The exception was Company B's office in Dublin, in a historic building with wood beams and floors; it felt warm and inviting and, of all the offices, I felt this was the one I'd most like to work in. I didn't want to leave and found it to be a great space for writing up field notes. While this feeling I got was based on my interaction across different offices of the same company, many employees hadn't been to other offices in other cities, so their feelings about the office space were based solely on their experience in London, Dublin, Sydney, San Francisco, and so on.

The companies in this study are spread out over the globe. They are considered in the press, social media, and pop culture. But they are corporations. Foster's writing about the anthropology of corporations influenced my own work when he says that ethnographic research (with corporations) would involve "interacting with informants across a number of dispersed sites, not just in local communities, and sometimes in virtual form; and it means collecting data eclectically from a disparate array of sources in many different ways [such as] formal interviews . . . extensive reading of newspapers and official documents . . . careful attention to popular culture," as well as informal social events outside of the actual corporate office (Foster 2017, 116).

I adopted this approach to research in my own fieldwork with Company A and Company B. My research was both inside and outside these offices, following their food programs through every channel I could find including social media, popular books, and media as well as ethnographic "hanging out" and interviews. The point is to "resist the force with which the corporation has become a taken-for-granted feature of everyday life" (Foster 2017, 112).

I went to a place that was already in some sense "familiar" to me (I had worked in offices in London and the United States before) and attempted to make it strange by taking it as an object of ethnographic analysis. I also attempted to take the tech industry itself as a familiar-stance object: how many of us have come to accept the fact that we will continue to use these products for the foreseeable future?

CARE AND WORK

During my time in the offices, I reached out to employees in different depart-ments to try and understand what it was that they did all day. To be honest, at the end of their explanations, I still struggled to grasp what kept them so busy, but what I did understand was that their jobs included a lot of meetings, phone calls and video conferences, spreadsheets, and, if you were an engineer, writing code. The legal and sales teams had clear tasks (managing contracts, selling the product); others had less-clear tasks. Tasks are a specialty of Melissa Gregg (here speaking to Gershon), who tells us that "task management through our devise is becoming obligatory" and that oftentimes software gives us elegant ways to do things without ever drawing attention to what we're doing or why (Gershon 2018).

Some of the jobs in the industry are ambiguous and this, as Graeber points out in his treatise *Bullshit Jobs,* can cause what he calls "spiritual violence" because the "worst thing about a bullshit job is simply the knowledge that it's bullshit" (Graeber 2018, 113). While none of the employees I spoke with classified their jobs as bullshit, people did mention that free food becomes an important part of their job and workday. Graeber doesn't consider the fact that free food might be enough to get some employees through the door in the morning. Some engineers, as we'll see later, might even choose companies based on the food they provide.

But what connects Graeber's job theory to this study is his consideration of care. Jan English-Lueck has been conducting research in Silicon Valley for years and her insight into the concept of care, and why care exists, is extremely important to understand—especially when free food is placed into this kind of categorization as opposed to something like a "perk" or "benefit." This links back to the phrase coined by Robbins as the "anthropology of the good" (Robbins 2013, 447). English-Lueck says:

> Providing care onsite, such as providing gyms and trainers, massage, and meditation guides and of course, food, changes the relationship of workers and those who provide their care. As with 20th century provisions, such care is not ubiquitous, or consistent. Many companies offer little to their employees, nothing to their contractors. Others offer a range of care practices, but charge fee-for-service; charges vary with the status of the worker. However, the notion of embedded, on-site care, hints at an experiment for broader worker-employer engagement, a moral contract. (English-Lueck and Avery 2014, 39)

This kind of moral contract, I argue, has some roots in an economic morality based on what Graeber calls a "baseline communism" where there are certain things shared or made freely available within the group and "others that anyone will be expected to provide for other members on request that one would never share with or provide to outsiders" (Graeber 2011, 116). This is opposed to exchange, which is based on equivalence across difference. At least in the ways that English-Lueck considers care, there can never be a true equivalence between the work being done and the care being given. Instead, when there are groups of people who see themselves as part of the group, the obligation to share food and other basic necessities within that group becomes the basis for an everyday morality (Graeber 2011, 114).

Over the course of thirteen months, observing office spaces and dining areas inside two companies, I encountered a lot of care that took the form of free food, drinks, snacks, coffee, and treats. What I discovered is that food matters to the employees of tech companies in myriad ways; it's used as a recruitment tool, as a reward, to build community, as a financial health indicator, as punishment, and as a topic of conversation. It isn't guaranteed in contracts but is an assumed perk or benefit; it goes without saying. It is part of the culture of the industry. Understanding the importance of food in the tech industry, then, helps us to recognize the mundane day-to-day social patterns of the office and work life and the more unusual events in the company and its culture (Strangleman 2010) and understand the social life of the tech office.

Office Spaces

Let's take a closer look at the Company A office in London. Kim welcomed me the first day in the office. She had long blond hair and blue eyes and was very tall—she was in her late twenties or early thirties. She spoke with the slightest Irish accent, which I couldn't help thinking must have been influenced by her training as an actress: she told me that working there as the office manager was her day job and gave her the flexibility to attend auditions and shoots when necessary. Acting had been a hard path, she said, but she did have a minor part in a season of *Game of Thrones*. "That sounds promising," I replied. Kim's role as the office manager entailed a number of tasks:

- receiving guests and managing appointments
- answering the door, greeting guests, receiving deliveries and mail
- managing kitchen snacks, ordering, and replenishing
- scheduling meetings for the director
- managing the food budget (including lunches twice a week and snacks/drinks/coffee)
- acting as the semi-official party organizer for office events and outings
- generally fielding all questions that no one seems to know who has the answer for

Kim combined feminized roles of care—her role in some ways resembled that of a traditional receptionist—with organizing the food. She dressed in a variety of ways but seemed to have two main outfits—yoga pants and active wear or more professional looking outfits that include pencil skirts and blouses or skinny jeans, flannel/plaid shirts, and a hat. This is not really the tech uniform, which I discuss later. Rather, her self-presentation was decidedly that of an urban office support worker and she would have looked at home in a number of offices.

Many of the people who manage the financial and logistical aspects of the food programs in tech offices are women, and all of them I spoke with and observed were. This could be reflective of the cultural notion of food service or providing food as comfort/care as women's labor, but my sense is that is a subconscious preoccupation with care that can't be brought into a hiring practice for reasons of discrimination. These employees do much more than just order food, though, which begs the question of what is the difference between a secretary or office manager and a food program manager. Sometimes, there isn't a difference, or the jobs overlap. They are often the go-to person for questions about HR, other benefits, or just getting set up on your first day. Maria, one of the employees in London, had this to say about her office manager, Kim:

Maria: She definitely holds the place together and also, every time she's away, it's just chaos. Not really chaos, you just notice the many things nobody takes care of, like putting the lunches correctly, like the groceries arrived and, obviously, nobody is responsible, nobody touches it. Unless Andrew will find some time and then he does it, but, obviously, his role is different as well. It would've taken probably ten minutes if we all sit together and did it.

Int: So, when she is on holiday . . . ?

Maria: Things are a little bit rougher, yeah. Rougher or just like the fridge hasn't been . . . She's not cleaning, that's not her job, but nobody puts the milk back where it belongs, little things like maintenance.

Int: So, you sort of notice the things that she does when she's not here to do them, I guess?

Maria: Oh, yeah, definitely. I don't know if it's only me.

Int: No, it's not only you.

Maria: No, she's great anyways.

Int: How do you think of her then?

Maria: Even though she's not, from the looks and the personality, but then it kind of is the mother figure in the office.

Int: She's the first person you go to if you have a problem if you don't know who to ask, if you don't know how . . .

Maria: Oh, yeah, of course. Yeah. "Can I have a Band-Aid?"

The office where Maria and Kim worked was bright. It was the first thing I noticed when I entered—that and the Ping-Pong table. There were a lot of windows, which allowed for natural light and a view of Charterhouse Square. The square is an English garden type of space complete with flowers, carefully tended grass, and a wrought iron fence. Across the lawn was the Charterhouse—a beautiful stone building housing a community called the "Brothers." The building and chapel were completed in 1611 and while I was conducting my fieldwork in the office, Queen Elizabeth II attended a ceremony in the chapel. The entire square was shut down to traffic and many of us from the Company A office went outside to see her and Prince Phillip arrive. On good days, the sun would cut through the windows and make the office even brighter, but the opposite was true as well—when the weather was bad (which it often is in London) then the fluorescent tubes in the ceiling came to the fore: bright but not warm.

All the walls were painted white, the desks were white, and the flooring was soft grey carpeting—the kind that can be walked on again and again. This color scheme gave everything a slightly antiseptic feeling. Immediately on the left from the entry were four glass-enclosed meeting rooms. There was a dividing wall straight in front of the door, which was white, but painted on it was the Company A logo with four vertical lights hanging in front of it. It divided the entryway from the sales team. There was an L-shaped wooden bench, a sofa, and a small table with two lounge-style chairs. Directly behind this wall was a closet, where some people hung their coats and which was also used for storage. Following that were two rows of desks where the sales team sat. To the left of this area and behind was another row of desks, again, more sales team.

Figure 1.1.   L to R: Microwave, coffee machine, toaster, and small fridge at Company A, London. Company A Office, London. Company A Office, London.

Moving on around the corner, there was a kid's swing, a beanbag, and a small round table with four "standard" chairs around it. There was a small cabin that had soundproofing foam in it, with a standing desk, where people could go to make phone calls and not let the sound carry throughout the office space. Yet the "room" had no door. I found this very odd but saw employees use it all the time and I never heard them, so it must work.

Continuing, you come to the desk where the office and technology managers sat along with the field operations employees. Again, the desks were white, with grey felt-covered dividers, and on each desk was a computer monitor and a phone. Behind them are the main printer and copy machine, which didn't get a lot of use. The copy machine was large and grey, and seemed to be excessive for an office of that size.

The next set of desks included mine, the lawyer, and the EMEA director. The desks were the same as the others. The desks were not in a line, but divided into four, two spaces on each side. To my left was the kitchen. There was a window in the far wall in the kitchen, which looked out into a lane and the bricks of the building next door. There was a white table under the window. It was here that the lunches were set when they were delivered. To the right of the window was a microwave. On top of the microwave was salt, pepper, hot sauces, sugar, napkins, paper towels, and bread for toast. To the right of that were a toaster and a large coffee machine.

Under the microwave was a refrigerator, which had milk, yogurt, and the food people brought themselves (which usually amounted to a random smattering of store-purchased yogurts and leftovers). Next to that was a clear glass drinks fridge. This was refilled weekly with a wide variety of options (from Coke and Diet Coke to juice and energy drinks). To the right of that was a dishwasher, which was filled and emptied almost exclusively by the cleaning lady twice a day. To the right of that was a heated cutlery drawer. The heated cutlery drawer was a surprise to me. I had never seen one before and have never come across one again. It seemed an odd thing to have in an office kitchen and I asked about it, but no one knew why it was there. To the right of that was a snack tower, where there was a big basket of fruit that was

Figure 1.2. The kitchen at Company A, London. To the right is a hallway that leads to the toilet and the locked closet.

delivered once a week as well as bags of popcorn, granola bars, and, on top, a cookie jar.

In the kitchen was a long table with seating benches on both sides. Next to that was a recycling bin and a general rubbish bin. On top of the table were pretzels, yogurt-covered raisins, nuts, pistachios, and gummy candies—all with small scoops for people to take however much they wanted.

Figure 1.3.   A view of the office manager's desk, the front door, and a foosball table. Also, the printer, copy machine, and windows that look out at the building next door.

Heading out of the kitchen, to the right, was a small hallway, which had been constructed with a wooden partition that was open at the top. Outside the door in the hallway are the stairwell and toilets. This door was locked, and access required an employee badge. I was given a guest badge with which to access this door and the front door to the office. At the end of the hallway was a closet where the physical things like ticket readers are kept (this door was always locked).

Moving down toward the other end of the office, there were three more banks of desks containing marketing, communication, and the account managers. To the left of the office manager's desk was an area with beanbags and a high cafe table, with stools, used mostly to fill space. Next to that area was another small meeting room, which was not used often because it was either too hot or too cold. This space was useful for me, though, because it was usually free, so I conducted a few cold interviews in there—during one, I wore my winter coat and scarf.

There is no specific space reserved for guests. Most of them are met at the door with the offer of a drink and are brought into a meeting room. There was no real discernible smell to the office (unless food was being warmed up or had just been delivered). Food was delivered twice a week using a service called City Pantry. City Pantry, itself a tech company, connects offices with catering services and restaurants. Kim communicated with an account manager there and together they planned the meals for the office a month in advance. Usually, Kim took into account any feedback from the employees and tried as much as possible to not be repetitive.

When the food arrived, hopefully as close to noon as possible, Kim unloaded it from the large thermal boxes onto the table in the kitchen and employees were free to help themselves whenever they liked (as we'll see, this is very different than what happens at Company B).

There was usually music playing from several speakers around the office—the music was managed by Kim or Andrew, the IT manager who sits at the desk next to Kim. The ambient temperature was comfortable, hovering around 20 degrees Celsius. It was nice that the windows opened to allow fresh air to circulate.

This was the basic layout of the Company A office in London and in some ways, it represents a kind of typical office space for a successful London tech company. It was not that much different from other offices I have personally worked in. It was not as grandiose as the tech offices I encountered in San Francisco, and it was not as comfortable as the Company B office in London, but it was in a prestigious part of town. It shows how space in these offices can either enhance food programs or diminish them: in this instance, there was a lack of space for everyone in the office to eat together. It also shows the disparity between offices in a global company in terms of the kinds and degree of "care" offered. While Kim's maternal role was a striking gesture at care, it was a long way from the Company A headquarters in San Francisco, where there was the option to do yoga, visit the doctor, or even use the smoothie room to blend up your own protein shake. In these global companies, those working in the "satellite offices" outside of the headquarters are often left out of the majority of the benefits, perks, and care that employees can experience in Silicon Valley itself. This, too, is a matter of space: there is a geography to the tech industry where San Francisco is the hub and apex, as aspirational place, where offices have bike parking and showers, nursing rooms for new mothers, and multiple types of coffee. The distribution of food and other forms of corporate care in these global companies confirmed this geography and repeated the message that Silicon Valley is the mecca of the industry.

Corporate Culture

Tech companies use multiple tools in their deployment of corporate culture, but three stand out as the most central. The first is the use of myths and mission statements, such as the debunked idea that YouTube's original idea came from two friends who were frustrated while trying to upload a video to the web of a party. The second is the onboarding process, and the third is food. The corporate mission statement (what I call a myth) is a necessary part of creating a company and a strong brand.[5] Through the careful use of mission statements, many of these companies have created a shared set of "values" or "core principles."

Articulating the relationship between myths and social practice, Malinowski writes that "an intimate connection exists between the word, the mythos, the sacred tales of a tribe, on the one hand, and their ritual acts, their moral deeds, their social organization, and even their practical activities, on the other" (Malinowski 1948, 96). Tech companies use myths as a way to evoke feelings of attachment to the company, regardless of the fact that many employees don't fully buy into the myths themselves. It is part of the cultural fit, that at least you have to buy into the myth to work here.

The notion that mission statements are myths is not a novel insight (as my endnotes show). But it is a key idea when considering corporate cultures. Tech companies have "invented traditions" just like most cultural settings do, and the mission statement is a key part of the invention of a corporate culture—using the materials at hand in the existing cultural setting in a novel way that answers the demands of the present (Hobsbawm and Ranger 1984). D'Costa says:

> Businesses, if they have a culture, may have a subculture (and it should not be assumed that they do have a culture)—but they ultimately answer to the main-stream cultural ethos. (D'Costa 2017)

Free food, open floor plans, and unlimited LaCroix sparkling water are benefits, not culture. What many of these tech companies believe they are creating are unique work cultures that reflect either

1. The vision and ideals of the founders (in smaller or privately held companies), or
2. An idealist version of what the company aims to achieve.

Even tech companies that have had much less impact on the world than Facebook still usually have mission statements that suggest their goal is to have a radical impact on the world. Company A's mission statement is "Bringing the World Together through Live Experiences." While this sounds simple and admirable, if taken literally it is also an ambition of considerable grandeur. Company B's is "Keep Commerce Human." Again, the simplicity belies the extremity of the ambition: can a tech company involved in e-commerce also single-handedly keep commerce human?

Onboarding is the process by which new employees are introduced to the company—it usually takes place within the first days in the office. Martinez calls it "seductive propagandizing" (Martinez 2016) and D'Costa says that "people may align themselves with company objectives simply because they need a job, and not because they have whole-heartedly bought into the company mission statement" (D'Costa 2017). The onboarding processes that I went through were modest. At Company B, I was given a small, branded bag filled with more branded items like a pencil, a notebook, and some stickers. I got tours of the offices. I was always shown how to use the coffee machines. I never saw any employees wearing a Company B T-shirt or a Company A T-shirt, though that's not to say they didn't exist. At Company A, I wasn't given anything and was given the requisite tour, complete with coffee machine and emergency exits.

But for long-term employees, especially in San Francisco, the onboarding process can be intensive. Martinez recounts a firsthand experience of how these companies invest in selling the myth to employees during the on-boarding. Onboarding is a critical moment for the company, and worth a closer look. It is not just the moment when companies must show the new employee that they are organized but, as Martinez and others have noted (at least those who are critical of the industry), it is the moment when you must "drink the Kool-Aid" so to speak. It's when you have to buy into the narrative that the company is spinning—you have to accept the stories and myths, at least to some degree, and sometimes even physically show that you are part of the group by wearing the company T-shirt or hat. While I did not receive the same kind of onboarding sessions when I started in the offices and I was not privy to any extreme onboarding procedures, as described by Martinez at Facebook (and my impression is that Facebook's extremes were not matched by the offices I spent time in), Martinez's description shows the investment that some companies make in inculcating company mythology into employees including daylong sessions in a room with a stage and receiving their personal devices and T-shirts and other branded objects to signal their "in-status" (Martinez 2016, 260–64).

Employees at Company A reported that usually within the first month of employment, they would get to go to the headquarters in San Francisco for anywhere between one and three weeks. While this might represent a form of training, I argue that it also has a symbolic dimension. Going to the headquarters meant glimpsing the mecca. Among other things, these new employees saw the amounts and kinds of food that employees in San Francisco had access to (as well as other perks and benefits not available in London). While this could have been a potential point of conflict or jealousy, no one recounted it like that to me. Company B employees did not receive trips to the headquarters as induction like Company A employees, but sometimes had the chance to go to the headquarters in Brooklyn for meetings, usually between two to five days long. Physical time spent in the headquarters of the company, then, is one way that companies build and transmit a sense of their unique corporate culture.

Another way is through food. And the kind of food served can say a lot about the larger goals of the company. At Company A, the food was fast, accessible, varied in terms of how healthy it was, and not particularly focused on the quality. At Company B, it was locally sourced, organic, focused on quality over quantity, and also very expensive. The two companies had two different ethoses and these were partly communicated through the food program and in reality, these two different food cultures reflect the companies themselves, one being more focused on access (to their product) and the other focused more on quality and "artisan" aspects of their business.

Sharing a meal is an excellent way to build community and promote collaboration. The concept of commensality is essential to this study and understanding the social dimensions of these offices. As we will see, it has multiple variations, additions, subtractions, mutations, and forces all its own (Morrison 1996, Sutton 2004, Ochs and Shohet 2006, Fischler 2011). I observed a lot of distractions that kept people from eating together at times—meetings, for one, often encroached into the lunch hour. But for the most part, I was consistently impressed with the number of employees who would stop what they were doing and sit down to their lunch together.

> Yeah, I really like it. I think it will be a big shock if I'm somewhere else that didn't have it. It definitely makes people sit together at lunch a lot more [in a] place where a lot of people used to eat at their desk. It definitely brings you all together at lunch, which is a really nice thing. It gets you away from your desk. (Nate, employee, Company A, London)

> For one, it's probably just a really good perk and something, a good starting point in the interview process on top of all the other benefits, because it's a good company. But I'm sure you lose time going out for lunch, queuing somewhere, getting lunch, or even eating it outside and coming back, so I think it's also a little bit motivating for us to maybe stay at work and even if you're busy, you still don't take the time to leave the office and then come back when you really have to be there at your desk. (Katie, employee, Company A, London)

What is often overlooked in studies that concern food and commensality are that food can also work to divide people and in these offices there were several ways in which food divides, although they take some focused attention to understand (Strangleman 2010). The divisions tended to be either gender divisions, team/work group divisions, or food habit divisions (e.g., vegetarians or vegans). These social inequalities were not so obvious in all of the field locations, but were very apparent in San Francisco, where the division was less about dividing employees internally, than it was about dividing the people on the "urine-soaked streets" with those in the offices.

Food program managers must deal with a number of food aversions or allergies. Some of the more common ones are vegetarians (no meat), vegans (no animal products at all), gluten-free, and allergies to foods like nuts, shellfish, and mustard. The offices I worked in tried to cater to all diets, although this was not always to the satisfaction of office workers: the number of vegetarians in London seemed to fluctuate from month to month. In San Francisco, vegans complained that there wasn't enough choice at mealtimes.

In addition, the food programs create social bonds between companies and employees: the food is given from one to the other. As Graeber says about small, less impersonal communities: "It is often difficult to refuse a request not just for tobacco, but for food—sometimes, even from a stranger; certainly, from anyone considered to belong to the same community" (Graeber 2014a, 69). If we take gifts to be "a way of creating social relations" as Graeber suggests, then free food can be understood as part of the ongoing onboarding process whereby employees are integrated into the corporate culture (Graeber 2001, 210).

Mauss said that "a gift is received with a burden attached" (Mauss 1990) and there is an obligation to accept the gift and to make a return. Derrida has questioned this understanding of the gift, arguing that Mauss misunderstood gifts if he believed they must be returned: the only true gift is one that is truly free. The true gift, according to Derrida, is "the unconditional gift, the one that is entirely gratuitous, and the gesture of which is not suspended on the condition of some context, or some proximity or family tie, be it general or specific" (Derrida 1992, 17).

Graeber has argued that in fact the idea that gifts must be returned has existed only at certain times and places in human history: it is not a universal idea, but it is a very strong idea in societies that are strongly hierarchical. Graeber understands the Maussian idea of gifts as part of a complex re-grounding "debt" in state-based societies: the idea that everything, even one's own life, is already owed contributes to people assuming and accepting submissive roles. This is especially so in societies where the idea of "tit-for-tat" is still explicitly taught as the epitome of good manners ("do unto others as you would have them do unto you").

Mauss's insights, then, continue to have relevance not as a general statement (such as "there is no such thing as a free gift") but as an observation of how many societies, including our own, understand freedom and obligation. On one hand, we have strong concepts of the gift as encompassing expressions of love, friendship, and respect. On the other hand, we have the less noble ideas of gifts as implying manipulation, flattery, bribery, deception, humiliation, domination, offense, and conflict (even death, in Mauss's examples). That a gift can be meant to kill is most clearly illustrated in the double meaning of the German (and Dutch) word "gift," which also means "poison."[6] In my observations of free food in the office, I saw this full range of understandings of the gift of food: there were notions of manipulation and bribery and these worked in tandem with the more positive aspects of gifting as care and nurture.[7] This resonated with an emerging theme in the anthropology of the gift: that the lived experience of gifts can be ambiguous, vacillating between the positive valences of gifting and the negative ones. But how would we consider gifts when we consider the workplace as home? As a place of refuge, sustenance, or support?

NOTES

1. On a side note, I learned a few things about online etiquette during this process. For one, I found that emails sent on a Sunday night had a higher chance of being read and responded to than any other day of the week, and that I needed to write emails like a tech employee—that is, short, to the point, almost like a text message. Long, explanatory emails went nowhere and were never read or responded to.

2. Because of these non-disclosure forms, I must withhold any further specific details about these companies.

3. https://www.employeebenefitslive.co.uk/about-us/about-eb-live.

4. If you do a search for Ping-Pong tables and tech companies, it is clear that I am not the first person to note this piece of "furniture." A sampling of article titles includes "Does Your Office Need to Ditch the Ping Pong Table?," "Why Ping Pong Tables Don't Lead to Greater Employee Engagement," "Ditch Those Ping Pong Tables and Embrace the Real Workplace of the Future," "What Is Your Company Culture Missing? It's Not a Ping Pong Table."

5. See https://medium.com/swlh/hacking-a-corporate-culture-stories-heroes-and-rituals-in-startups-and-companies-4913c05e7820, https://www.theatlantic.com/magazine/archive/2006/06/the-management-myth/304883/, https://www.fastcompany.com/1298657/corporate-creation-myths-and-why-we-need-them, https://www.businessinsider.com/whats-your-creation-myth-2011-5?IR=T, and https://martinroll.com/resources/articles/branding/identity-myths-storytelling-keys-building-iconic-brands/.

6. From the online etymology dictionary: Gift: c. 1200, "a deadly potion or substance," also figuratively, from Old French *poison, puison* (12c., Modern French *poison*) "a drink," especially a medical drink, later "a (magic) potion, poisonous drink" (14c.), from Latin *potionem* (nominative *potio*) "a drinking, a drink," also "poisonous drink" (Cicero), from *potare* "to drink" (from PIE root *$*po(i)$*- "to drink"). For form evolution from Latin to French, compare *raison* from *rationem*. The Latin word also

is the source of Old Spanish *pozon*, Italian *pozione*, Spanish *pocion*. The more usual Indo-European word for this is represented in English by *virus*. The Old English word was *ator* (see *attercop*) or *lybb* (cognate with Old Norse *lyf* "medicinal herbs"; see leaf (n.)). Slang sense of "alcoholic drink" first attested 1805, American English.

7. Graeber points out that in some cases, no reciprocity is expected between unequal people and in fact, the person of lesser status might ask for more next time, which only works to reduce his status (Graeber 2001).

Chapter Two

Workplace as Home

LEARNING HOW TO BE A TECH EMPLOYEE

It was 9:30 a.m. on a stark morning in London. Inside the Company A office, it was warm; the bright overhead lights shone into our eyes. Employees arrived a bit later than normal. I was in the kitchen making a coffee when Maria, an early thirties Polish employee with long brown hair, joins me. She works as an account manager,[1, 2] mostly for the German market. She sits a few rows ahead of my desk and faces the white, bare wall. There are four other women working around her, all in similar bland workstations.

I made small talk about the commute this morning and how cold it felt outside. She filled her Instagram page with images of trips to warm climates, destinations near the sea, lounging in her garden, or going out for dinner. Her experience in London was positive, she assured me, but left her longing for something else. "The long winter gets to you, even if it's never as bad as Poland," she said. Maria became a key informant during my research and one of the few employees I have been able to keep track of. Her experience as a Polish employee, for an American company, in an office in London resembles a very *meta*, modern way of living and working: international, global, integrated. That is, it resembles a global type of employee that can live and work nearly anywhere. Before working at Company A, Maria held jobs with FIFA, the soccer consortium. She mentioned one day that she hoped to take a sabbatical from Company A in order to work for the upcoming World Cup in Russia.[3]

There were days in the field where I didn't really know if I would actually like to have a job like Maria's. Early on, I scribbled notes like "I'm not sure what these people do all day or how they are feeling about it when they go home?" Their own feelings about work, life, families, and how to balance it all did come out during conversations, during impromptu coffee breaks, and at the pub after work. I'm not saying that I didn't eventually understand the disenfranchisement that some feel, the isolation, or the feeling that it's just a job like any other. The thoughts and feelings of employees came through loud and clear. And it's not that I feel like I didn't connect with them: at the end of my time there, many of them felt like friends. It's that the tech industry, at least these companies, created a feeling of disconnect and alienation. This was a major ethnographic lesson. Sitting in an open plan office, surrounded by others, felt surprisingly lonely at times. This is all the more startling when my purpose was to study food, commensality, and the free meals employees receive.

Some of the other personalities I encountered included an aspiring actress, an author who was actively working on a second book, a programmer with a PhD from Stanford, an opera singer, a teacher, a former agriculture labor organizer, a would-be baker, a long-distance swimmer, a near-retirement age lawyer with small children, a former English major who was good at Excel, angry people, happy people, disillusioned people. I watched, listened, asked, entertained, ate, drank, helped, photographed, recorded, walked, ran, laughed, and tried to understand them, the jobs they did, the industry they work in and why, how, and to what extent free food played a role in their career.

What I realized is that tech companies are not as strange as we think they are; they are stranger. The technology industry as a whole can be hard to grasp from the outside because many companies are not involved in making physical things. Apple has it easy—they make products you can touch. But most tech companies don't. Neither of the two companies described here produce anything physical.

I use Apple as the comparison because they are primarily in the business of building computers, phones, and other goods—they have factories, rely on raw materials from a number of countries around the world, and bring them all together to create the very computer I'm writing on now. Company A and Company B, though, represent the other side of the tech industry—one where the goods are not as easily seen, where the product is not made out of raw materials.[4] This is a side of the industry that is integrated into our lives as much as an Apple computer, but in a different way. Apps, websites, and products like Company A, are purely digital. They rely on the internet to facilitate their use—without the internet, there is no way for Company A to function. Similarly, with Company B, without the internet, there is no way for this company to continue to operate. What I encountered is a side of the industry that sometimes, if not always, forgets that the backbone of their business is built on the physical technology of the internet—switches, boards, cables, lines, satellites, and electricity.

Then there are satellite offices. I use the term "satellite," but they could also be called remote offices or international offices (there is no real industry-standard term). These terms refer to offices of a company that are not the headquarters. What I found inside these spaces was a slightly slower pace, although still long hours, a different mentality about how work and non-work time should interact, and, of course, differences in the kind, quality, and quantity of free food and drinks employees in these offices were given. Satellite offices are particularly interesting because they can show us how a company culture either functions on top of the local culture or is somehow integrated into it. Erin Griffith has written about work in the United States, and specifically about the work culture in San Francisco, saying that "techies here have internalized the idea—rooted in the Protestant work ethic—that work is not something you do to get what you want; the work itself is all" (Griffith 2019).

Work hours are a good way to explore the different ways organizational culture interacts with local cultures in satellite offices. In the United Kingdom, there are "maximum weekly working hours." The UK government website clearly states: "You can't work more than 48 hours a week on average. You can choose to work more by opting out of the 48-hour week."[5]

Exceptions are provided for the following roles:

- Where twenty-four-hour staffing is required
- In the armed forces, emergency services, or police
- In security and surveillance
- As a domestic servant in a private household
- As a seafarer, sea-fisherman, or worker on vessels on inland waterways
- Where working time is not measured and you're in control, for example, as a managing executive with control over your decisions

None of the roles in the tech offices corresponded to the list of exceptions, except for the last, which I think would include creatives and even programmers who usually have control over their own time. This is an example where the local culture (or law) of a country overrules that of the company. The tech industry has created a culture that supports and rewards long hours. But in the United Kingdom, unless you waive your right to not work more than forty-eight hours, you don't legally have to—although I suspect that in some offices and workplaces, there is not much of a choice. This does not take into account how that might affect your promotion or your relationships with your team in the office. What it doesn't take into account is what does it mean to be working and who is keeping track? Most, if not all, employees I talked to gave an estimate of their weekly work hours—no one kept an exact count. So, proving that you work more or less than forty-eight would prove difficult.

IMPRESSIONS OF THE FIELD

Fog was a common sight on my commute from Berkeley. I took the BART, the Bay Area's metro-like train, for about thirty minutes into the heart of the city and walked a few blocks to the Company A office. The first thing the receptionist gave me was a name badge. The second was a key to a locker followed by a quick tour of the office (these tasks would have been done by an office manager in a satellite office). The sprawling floor was organized in a giant square, with a large dining area in the middle filled with snacks and drinks with two more "rungs" of space around the center. Each corner of the space was occupied by a different team or group of workers. Engineering in one corner, sales in another, product and operations in a third, and in the fourth overflow, art/design, and marketing. On what I'll call the second ring of space, there were meeting rooms and breakout spaces, all outfitted with flat screen televisions and video conferencing setups. Some of these rooms were small, accommodating two or three people, and some were larger, holding up to ten or twelve. Some had no doors at all and featured just a comfortable chair like you might find in a hotel lobby, with a lamp and a small table. The center of the space was the food area. This was busier than the second ring of space. A wall of snacks featured over sixty-three types of food, twelve kinds of hot sauce, a coffee bar with barista who made a full range of espresso drinks, a smoothie room offering ten different kinds of fruit and vegetables to include in your own blended smoothie (it was closed off from the rest of the office because of the noise generated by the Vitamix blenders), a breakfast nook with twelve different cereals, a basket of fruit, a fridge with soy/almond/ dairy milks, seven kinds of yogurt, and three fridges full of drinks—twenty-six different varieties including everything from Diet Coke to energy drinks to a plethora of options of LaCroix sparkling water. I'll note that also in the drinks fridges were non-dairy creamer in two different flavors.

It was an overwhelming amount of choice for an office. A few days in, standing on the fourth floor of the office building, looking out one of the large windows to the east toward hazy hills, I could see a long line of cars on the freeway headed into town. I felt alone and out of place in this office of three hundred. No one noticed me—some maybe assumed I was just another employee they didn't know. My picture and introduction had been sent around to everyone before my arrival, but it seemed to make no impact: maybe people were too busy to read their emails or just didn't care about or didn't want to take part in my project. Or perhaps they were just too busy.

I thought of home, which felt a very long way away. On the one hand, the alienation I was feeling was the furthest thing from my idea of home, but on the other hand, this office seemed incredible homey compared to other offices

I had known. In this office, you could eat most of your meals, pick up your dry cleaning, visit a doctor, and even take a nap in a sleeping pod or in the nap room. It had showers provisioned with toiletries. It had all the conveniences of home, and indeed many more. All of this makes the office seem like a place you can spend a lot of time in, perhaps even make into your second home. Indeed, as I got to know people there better, I found that many of them relied on the office for homey comforts which they no longer maintained at home: one employee said she didn't bother to buy her own fresh vegetables anymore, as they only rotted in fridge in her apartment. Her work had come to fill some of what might once have been a feature of her home. Yet, looking out that window on that day, I felt out of place and unsure how to reach out to anyone. I went to my desk and started working, just like everyone else with my head down and a cup of coffee next to my notebooks.

The number of perks that epitomize domestic life in these organizations is growing. In *The Anthropology of Busyness*, anthropologist Charles Darrah discusses how busy families in Silicon Valley manage their lives (Darrah 2007). Focusing on employees with families, instead of single employees right out of college, Darrah describes a view of busyness that is all-encompassing. In reference to my own work, it has been useful to see what employees in 2007, when he did the research, were given by the companies as opposed to what they are given now. Then, he mentions a laptop computer and an at-home internet connection. Considering the pieces of technology that my informants got from companies (an iPhone and a MacBook Air were the norm) as well as the added benefits that cover the more domestic aspects of life (childcare or an on-site doctor), Darrah's work shows how, in a very short amount of time, benefits and perks increased while busyness stayed the same or increased.

Google, for example, offers even more benefits than most, and some of these make it harder for some employees to imagine leaving. But do sleep pods, free meals, and having dogs in the office really make employees feel at home in the office? Amanda, a marketing specialist at Company B in London, told me that "this is the first company I've worked for that offers free food at work. At my previous company, I had to even bring in my own cutlery, coffee mug, and we had to pay for tea and coffee." In Amanda's experience, the answer seems to be that the experience of food in the office is a clear message about how welcome one feels—but she did not say that it made her feel more at home. Bringing your own mug has the benefit of a certain kind of homeyness (your own mug at least feels "yours") but there is the jarring sense that the mug is a reminder that you are not really being provided for: you are providing for yourself. You are welcomed here, but only in the sense that you are welcome to do your own thing and provide for yourself. The free food program at Company B, however, was a gesture of welcome in the sense of hospitality: this is our place, the food seemed to say, please make our home your home. Make yourself at home here.

Building Rapport through Footwear

When you're at home, you want to feel comfortable, and clothing has a lot to do with comfort. The dress code inside tech offices doesn't conform to any one standard, but it does give employees the opportunity to dress comfortably. I observed employees in what I consider pajamas and employees in high heels, suits, and everything in between. Saying that, it was rare to see someone in a suit and tie. Most of what I observed were variations on the jeans/T-shirt/sneakers theme. Age did not inhibit clothing choices so much as cultural capital. This form of cultural capital acts as a form of currency that aids in the navigation of the tech industry—the state of one's wardrobe indicates not just social class but, in this case, also industry (Crane and Bovone 2006, 323). The odd part about clothing choice is that, to many, the clothes or shoes standard in the industry might not appear to be expensive. For those in the "tribe," however, they signify being part of the group (Bourdieu 1984). This goes against Veblen's notion of conspicuous consumption in terms of lavish spending, but still sits firmly in the idea of consumption as affording a "taste of luxury/freedom" (Ochs et al. 1996, 7), where cultural capital assumes a distance from mere necessity. In *Chaos Monkeys,* Antonio Garcia Martinez takes note of the Silicon Valley wardrobe and describes one of his coworkers as wearing a button down shirt, cotton slacks in khaki, a slide belt, and Sperry Top Sider shoes with no socks (Martinez 2016, 128).

My own budget was small compared to the salaries of the employees I was surrounded by, yet this didn't prevent me from wearing what seemed right—I was comfortable in what I wore.

"Hey, nice Allbirds," I hear an employee say to me as she walks past. I looked down at my grey, 100 percent New Zealand wool sneakers, which I had bought just a few days before in a shop downtown. "Thanks," I said back—and she walked off. "What a strange comment," I thought, and went back toward my desk—what I should have done was ask her why she mentioned my shoes, but it didn't occur to me then. It was the first of three comments I heard within a month of buying the shoes.

Allbirds have become very popular in the tech industry. Worn by countless employees at all levels, I didn't immediately understand their importance. Only after did I come across the discussion by Bowles of Allbirds in the uniform-like dress of Silicon Valley. He says that standing out with personal style is "generally shunned" because it indicates time spent on aesthetic pursuits instead of work. "Tech-leaders" he continues, "settled on Allbirds" as part of their dress code, much like those in the venture capital class who, as Bowles says, "select investments in part based on who looks like them" (Bowles 2017). The shoes are to the tech industry (at least in 2017/2018) what the necktie seems to be for the financial industry. It's a signal, a sign: I'm one of you, I speak your language—we can do business together.

My shoes were inadvertently an entryway into conversations, casual interactions, and creating a sense of trust in the office because other people in the "tribe" recognized them. They are available online, but it seemed that more often than not, many bought them at the lone Allbirds store in downtown San Francisco. They are simple yet well made, without any logos or branding on them. They are comfortable, washable, ethical, and sustainable—words that tick all the right boxes for this group of high-status professionals. Shoes might not be a natural way to think about building rapport in a field site, but as Mats Alvesson says, at-home ethnography is "a study and a text in which the researcher-author describes a cultural setting to which s/he has a 'natural access' and in which s/he is an active participant, more or less on equal terms with other participants" (Alvesson 2009). These shoes helped me to be on more equal terms with the participants. I never once got a comment on the shoes outside of a tech office.

Fitting in is important, yet as Bowles says, personal style is generally shunned. So, if feeling at home means feeling good in what you choose to wear, feeling comfortable, what kind of pressure does this put on employees who do have a personal style they want to express? Matthew Crawford says, "The demand to be an individual makes us feel anxious, and the remedy for this, ironically enough, is conformity. We become more deferential to public opinion" (Crawford 2015, 195). The shoes relieve those who wear them, at least in the tech industry, of the possibility of being judged for their fashion choices: the tribe has chosen for everyone, so buy them and stop worrying. I realized I responded to this pressure too: if I wanted any chance of meeting participants and employees that wanted to talk to me, I couldn't show up in a suit. I'd surely be laughed out of the building. The constant tangle with feeling at home then extends to clothing. Wearing pajamas might be okay—it indicates a certain severity of work ethic in its own way (too busy to dress?)—but wearing Allbirds means you got the memo.

Felix Stein, in his book *Work, Sleep, Repeat,* takes the question of clothes into account in his study of German business consultants. In their extreme lifestyle of more-or-less constant travel, the peculiarities of their "tribe" almost fully determined their behavior—from "the food they ate to the clothes they wore and the ways they spoke" (Stein 2017, 178).

In the tech industry, there was a uniform-like pressure on clothing and also to have a free food program and indeed a utopian mission statement. These emerged from a complex and at times contradictory set of industry-wide values: there is a value placed on efficiency, hard work, and time spent in the office. But there are also those utopian goals, such as "do no evil." Wool rather than synthetic sneakers are part of the industry-wide value placed on ethical and sustainable decisions. This was evident in the food program, too, especially in the Californian offices where there was an emphasis on organic, sustainably produced, and locally sourced food. "California Cuisine" often stood next to sodas in disposable cans and snacks wrapped in brightly colored non-degradable plastics. There are contradictory goals in the industry, and these were expressed in some of the contradictions at the ubiquitous snack bar. The Allbirds represented a collective fantasy: even in the scurry of urban city life marked by long work hours, homelessness on the streets, and ener-vated home lives, we can still tread lightly on the earth.

Stein ponders the idea of home and field sites again, later in his book, where he asks, "Where and when are we in the field? If geography does not matter, then what are the main criteria that may allow us to define it?" (Stein 2017, 20). In his case, the field was messy—it was hotels, offices, hallways, taxis, airports, and airplanes. The field was everywhere and nowhere. Still, as a consultant, it was, in a way, his home. But far from being an advantage, this aspect contributed to creating some confusion. As he mentions later in the book, his main abode—the place where he kept his possessions—was rarely used. Like tech offices, work became the substitute home for employees, even if that wasn't just one space but a collection of many spaces. My home, while doing ethnographic research, was in many ways the same. A collection of spaces, from London to San Francisco—I did, at times, feel homeless, as if I was more like those on the streets below than those in the office. I felt the divide.

Thinking about Home[6]

Helene Brembeck has used the concept of home to try and understand how it is created for families, with a focus on meals had at McDonald's. In her paper "Home to McDonald's" she explores this idea in Sweden where she con-cludes that because McDonald's are places with meaning, value, joy, and so-ciality, they might even be "homes" for many families (Brembeck 2005). The challenge for the researcher is to find the exotic in the familiar (Ybema 2009, 2)—something that Kate Fox took to heart in her own research, chronicled in her book *Watching the English*. The first chapter is titled "Anthropology at Home." In researching her home country of England, she chronicles her pain by needing to break the very rules that she is setting out to understand—the rules she knows as an English woman, which include purposefully bumping into people in a train station to count the number of people who say sorry, and to then spend a few hours "queue jumping" (Fox 2004, 1).

When we enter our home field, we might feel like we have some sort of advantage while in fact we might have to, like Fox, break the rules of our own culture and society on purpose in order to understand their origins. I never did try turning up to a tech office in a suit. The social pressure was overwhelming: I didn't want to be seen as the odd one out, and I did not have the luxury of anonymity that she had working in public spaces. But I understand her point: that rules can be so pervasive that it takes some strenuous effort to perceive them, let alone break them. Working in these tech offices, I monitored myself for small cues about assumed rules—whose chair am I not meant to sit in? Who's always the first in line for lunch? Or, even simpler, what time do I arrive and leave? Jennifer, the food program manager at Company B in London, told me about her first day:

> I was so nervous about the shared meal at work on my first day. I didn't know where to sit or who to talk to. I just didn't want to step on anyone's toes—I didn't want to take their spot. So now, we've implemented this program across all the offices. New employees' first day is always a Tuesday, a meal day, and they eat with the food program manager. We show them how to do it. Then on Thursday, they eat with their manager and team. (Jennifer, employee, Company B, London.)

I, too, had to be inducted into the norms of each food program I participated in. The first mistake I made in the Company A office was cleaning up my dishes after lunch. I had started to rinse my plate off and was about to put it in the dishwasher when an employee stopped me and said: "You don't need to do that; the cleaning lady will take care of it." Sure enough, about two hours later, a woman who works for the building came and cleared up any leftover food, put all the dishes in the dishwasher, swept the floor, and generally tidied up the kitchen. She arrived again just before everyone left to take care of any afternoon tea and coffee cups or plates that might have been used for an afternoon snack. These kinds of minor infractions were instrumental to my understanding of how to be part of the office environment. Even if I wasn't an employee, I was still somehow held to the same standards and expected to do as the others did. This particular incident also made me feel like a helpless child, as if a mom or dad would take care of cleaning up after a meal. If the food program is part of making a home environment, it is one that at times positions the employee in that home as a cared-for infant or dependent.

Doing ethnography at home, I believe, also gives you the ability to pay attention to micro-interactions. Like Fox, if you understand your own culture from a personal level, these micro-interactions (or infractions) are easier to spot; they make you uncomfortable. It's through these micro-interactions that we can begin to understand the effects of these institutions, companies, or field sites. Collins (2014) emphasizes this practice and Barley and Tolbert (1997) tell us that it is going out of fashion—more researchers are focused on the macro. But like the dining halls in Cambridge colleges, "the performance masks any conflict that may be present under the surface, giving the impression of a sophisticated social order that participants want to be associated with" (Dacin et al. 2010, 1394).

Offices are sophisticated social orders, perhaps not as ordered as a Cambridge college dining hall but ordered, nonetheless. There is a real sense of going back to a time where your mum (or parents) prepare your meal, clean up after you, take care of your laundry, and tell you what to wear. Included in these tech companies is also the idea of "play" or structured recreation, where Ping-Pong tables, scooters, video game rooms, and special meals or treats for celebrations enhance the startup culture. Is this representative of a type of organization that wants its employees to feel *like kids* at home? English-Lueck writes that "bigger tech companies or corporations—what they do to drive productivity is to try and eliminate the outside world" (English-Lueck and Avery 2017, 44). In other words, they create a home for employees.

When we talk about home, we don't mean the physical space where we keep our things. Rather, we refer to the concept of a home culture, which can be as specific as, say, a neighborhood or as broad as a country. Home is conceptual. It is imagined and idealized, yet it has been holding a powerful sway over people. What happens when the lines between home and work become blurred even more? I ate a lot of free meals during my research, but I never really felt at home there. So, this idea of the field and home is one that bounces around in my head—a concept that is more conceptual than actual.

Maybe your office feels comfortable because you have your own space that is private and closed off. In open plan offices, the lack of privacy can lead to a feeling of observation, which is exactly the opposite of being at home. Konnikova addresses this in "The Open-Office Trap" when she says that open offices remove an element of control which can lead to "feelings of helplessness" (Konnikova 2014). And she continues about younger workers who lack privacy and miss an ability to control their environment but who believe that the "trade-offs were ultimately worth it." They valued the time spent with coworkers and socializing.

The sense of camaraderie that Konnikova mentions could also be a result of commensality. Actually, the provision of free food and the ubiquity of the open plan office space seemed to work at odds with one another. Homes are private, cozy, intimate; these offices were not. The offices in which my research took place had a decisive lack of privacy. I found myself wondering if anyone noticed if I was reading the news on my computer as opposed to writing field notes or if I was a few minutes late, or if I left early. I felt monitored, even when in reality, I was not. The noise and lack of privacy was an acknowledged problem for productivity in these offices. Some employees booked conference rooms for themselves in order to get some work done without interruption. Food programs in these offices took place in a cultural use of space that meant that, often, people were already too much in one another's faces, ears, and mental space. People were brought together around food in a context where often what they would have liked was a little time alone, so they could get some work done.

Beyond leaving the field, a major challenge to the researcher in these globalized days is the understanding of where and what home is, and how a home can be conceived not just in terms of research but of actual stable living accommodation. The field site is meant to be, for those in anthropology, a place where you live amongst the community you are studying—as this arrangement is part of the concept of "immersion" into the field. What if you already live there? Does it mean that you are already immersed in the field site? Perhaps, but in such a way that demands that you step away—or at least separate yourself—from your research. A field is a funny place, full of characters, mystery, and the unknown. I once spoke with a colleague doing research on a cruise ship—a very odd place, if there ever was one. To him, it was far from what he considered home, but when he spoke with those who lived and worked on the ship, he found a different story. Home is relative.

Bourdieu found inspiration for his work at home, in France. Fox, too, found her research led her to look at her own culture more closely—at home. D'Costa is constantly looking at social and cultural oddities in her own culture—at home, in New York, or within the world of business (D'Costa 2017). Sherry Ortner has studied Hollywood, at her doorstep, yet a world away from her own community (Ortner 2010). Laura Nader talks about Berkeley students in the 1970s as studying "institutions and organizations that affect everyday lives, such as the California Insurance Commission or the Oakland Better Business Bureau"—all of which are "at home" in the Bay Area (Nader 1972).

Each one of them discovered something new and unique in studying at home, and this is reflected in their work. It's in this work that I initially took ideas and ways of constructing my field site—mentally, at first, and then physically when I was there. Their insights were key to my own awareness. But none of them seemed to deal with the process of being inside an organization that attempts to mimic home. None of them wrestles with the concept directly, preferring to stand at a distance to these topics, to observe from afar, it seems. Fox is perhaps the one who immersed herself to the fullest extent in her home, leaving her to experience issues of breaking the rules of English-ness that she was trying so hard to understand.

Fox's home is not necessarily where she keeps her things but is instead her home country. That is where she takes up her work. But it's worth mentioning here the idea that there have been a number of studies that showcase the dif-ferences between what men and women do in the home—housework. While the kinds of work done in these offices spaces is in some ways similar, in that these women are providing food and meals for people, the clear difference is that they are paid to do so. DeVault commits a number of pages to this topic, yet her analysis stands on the basis of household chores that are unpaid, split between genders or family units. Nonetheless, there is something to be said for the underlying idea that families (and employees) should eat together (DeVault 2013).

Some of this historical struggle will be seen later on when I discuss the field sites in San Francisco. It's with this feeling that "being at home" is both my methodology (fieldwork in my home countries) but also my subject of study (an office providing the comforts of home) that I returned again and again to the concept of home not just as cultural, but as personal and contex-tual, and a constantly shifting amalgamation of these. Home is physical as much as mental. Did I find myself at home in these organizations? Not neces-sarily. I did find aspects of home that I took comfort in while I was there. But upon leaving the field, reconnecting with my wife and my life, I realized that the organization would never be able to replicate home enough for any em-ployee. For all the perks and care that are provided, what organizations like tech companies lack are the deep feelings and personal connections to home that make it real. But to get to that point, the entire idea of feeding employees in tech had to start somewhere. And for that, we must take a look at Google, Charlie Ayers, and the idea of California Cuisine.

NOTES

1. An open position at Company A described the role in this way: "As Customer Success Manager, you will work with a diverse group of customers to drive a deep understanding of the goals for their business and engage them with our platform in a way that will ensure success. You will also work cross functionally to ensure that we are delivering the best solutions and strategies for our customers, giving them the knowledge, tools, and training they need to be successful, as well as articulating the value that Company A provides to their business."

2. This position is now known as a "customer success" manager.

3. Maria did end up getting time off from Company A to work for the World Cup in Russia and temporarily relocated to Moscow. I followed along on her Instagram account, and saw that when she got back to the C1 office in London she was welcomed with open arms, gifts, and signs saying, "Welcome home." I never asked her which job she liked the best, but in the end the World Cup is only every four years—one needs a steady job in between. C1 is a company that allows these types of breaks to happen, although, if you read the reviews on Glassdoor about time away and unlimited vacation, it sounds like taking time off from working in the San Francisco office is hard without feeling guilty or giving up leverage in advancement. Although Maria never expressed this to me, she has been promoted at C1 throughout her time with the company.

4. Some might say that "we," being people, are the product.

5. https://www.gov.uk/maximum-weekly-working-hours.

6. "Home" comes from the Old English word *ham* meaning "dwelling place, house, abode, fixed residence; estate; village; region, country," from Proto-Germanic **haimaz* "home" (source also of Old Frisian *hem* "home, village," Old Norse *heimr* "residence, world," *heima* "home," Danish *hjem*, Middle Dutch *heem*, German *heim* "home," Gothic *haims* "village").

Chapter Three

The Path to Free Meals

THE FIRST MEAL

It is unclear when exactly free food entered the tech industry. What is clear is that today, it is on a scale that none might have predicted. Google alone serves 175,000 meals a day around the world. The closest we can get to understanding how it all started seems to be with Charlie Ayers, the very first chef at Google, employee number 53. Ayers took his cooking cues from California Cuisine, a vague term that has come to encompass a number of ingredients like avocados and goat cheese and recipes like the California roll, California pizza, and Cobb salad. Chefs like Alice Waters led the way in the 1970s toward a different way of eating—a style based more on a European model of fresh, local, seasonal—now all trendy keywords that speak to elites. Yet Beriss argues that "before Alice Waters thought of the idea, chefs in New Orleans were building their menus around local ingredients, even as they sought to present themselves as representatives of high French style" (Beriss et al. 2007, 162). With the opening of Chez Panisse in 1971, Waters landed as the model of "Cali" food. The counter-culture movement of the 1960s and 1970s in San Francisco and the Bay Area not only changed politics and human rights agendas but gastronomic ones as well. Her restaurant, which is still open in Berkeley, remains a mecca for foodies from around the globe.

By the time Google was getting started, California Cuisine had become a mainstay in the Northern California culture. Ayers, talking on the Internet History podcast, mentions that during the cook-off to decide who would be Google's chef, he cooked foods that fit the profile of California Cuisine; he got the job. Using Wilk's definition of a cuisine as "a combination of foodstuffs, dishes, and meals that characterize a particular group of people, location, period, or corporate entity" (Wilk 2015, 241) it is easy to see how

California Cuisine and the food programs in Silicon Valley firms seem to go hand in hand.

My original plan was to conduct research inside Google's offices. That idea was never approved by Google management. But, since Google arguably has one of the largest and most visible free food programs in the industry, I needed to have at least some exposure to what was going on inside these dining spaces before entering smaller, more compact companies with less employees and smaller budgets. I found that getting invited to lunch was not very difficult: I put out a message on Facebook asking for introductions and ended up getting invited to two different offices. Here I'll talk about the Google office in Sydney, and later I will discuss lunch at Google's office in London. Both experiences helped to solidify ideas about tech companies, especially concepts about work/life balance, how food and food spaces are created and utilized, and how commensality comes into focus.

My first lunch at Google was at the office in Sydney. "Help yourself to whatever you want," my host, Miriam, said as we entered the cafeteria. I met Miriam through a friend of a friend with an email chain that runs into the double digits. She spent several years working at Microsoft before moving to Google's sales team several years ago. Her tour of Google's three buildings was fascinating. Every floor had micro-kitchens, complete with barista-style coffee machines and snacks that included fruit, nuts, muesli bars, chocolates, juice, packaged Asian-inspired crisps, and water, among other things. They were full and beautifully stocked, reminiscent of a Whole Foods Market—the space was open and there were low, trendy lighting, tables, and booths. It had the feel and smell of a restaurant and, with million-dollar views across to the Harbor Bridge, was not a bad place to eat.

As soon as you entered the dining area, there was a hot bar on the left where the cooked meals were being prepared. The day I went, it was seafood stew cooked in a rich, spicy tomato sauce, roasted chicken, brown rice, and steamed vegetables. Another station had Asian-inspired salads, prepared wraps, and a help-yourself salad bar.

The coffee counter had a long queue of people, like a cafe in the city. The baristas were taking orders and asking for names. Every conceivable option was available—soy, almond, skim, and whole milk, hot chocolate, and multiple kinds of tea. If you're going to sit in the dining area, real china cups are used. If you want to take it to your desk, or elsewhere, recyclable paper coffee cups are available. Next to the coffee bar was a smoothie and juice area, with piles of fresh fruit to combine into your own personal blend. On one table was a spot for the "daily special"—a rich chocolate tart with vanilla ice cream. By the time I finished my lunch and went back for a slice, there was none left. "It happens a lot. You have to be quick, especially with the desserts," said Miriam.

Figure 3.1.   The dining area and coffee bar at Google's office in Sydney.

After we sat down, and I explained my research, she said: "Of course, we all know that the food is to keep us in the office longer." This goes against what Google claims is the real reason for all the free food—Bock says, "Google isn't some sweetly baited trap designed to trick people into staying at the office working all the time" (Bock 2015, 275). But working all the time or hustling, or at least being connected, seems to be part of the tech workplace. I noticed that Miriam had sent me emails at various times of day, including late at night, early morning, and all times in between. Throughout our conversation, it became clear that she found it hard to define when her workday started, saying, "I don't know where my workday begins and ends. I'm constantly connected to the Google internal intranet and since it is a global company, I receive emails at all hours. I have to shut off my phone to be able to even consider that I'm done with work for the day." This is echoed in a recent book by Anne Helen Peterson which, in so many words, conveys the idea that disconnecting from work for some people is part of the problem—technology that had once promised ease instead has created dis-ease and contributed to burnout (Petersen 2020).

Free food at work might be one of the factors responsible for blurring the boundaries between work and private life, but it certainly is not the only one; technology is another major player. Miriam's experience shows that, even when they aren't getting free food, employees are still working long hours, unable to disconnect.

We toured the office spaces just past midday, and I did not see anyone eating at their desk, which I found odd. I asked her about this. "There really isn't any incentive to eat at your desk," she said. This division was more evident at Google than in other corporate offices I have visited, where dining areas functioned as workspaces and desks as makeshift dining tables. That said, it is difficult to say how many of the people eating together at Google were also having meetings.

We walked across the campus to another building where she claimed, "The food was better." She confirmed my suspicion that employees know where the best food is and tend to gravitate toward that location. This promotes cross-department interaction—one of Google's top goals. However, it is hard to know whether varying the food quality is intentional or not. She also mentioned that, after visiting other Google offices around the world, she realized that there were clear differences in the quality, quantity, and variety of the food served, all based on office size, local budgets, food cost, and overall availability. For example, Google's office in Auckland, New Zealand, is too small to host a food program; employees have a $25 daily food budget, which they can use in any given restaurant and expense to the company. This, of course, creates a very different office dynamic as compared to what I observed in Sydney and doesn't necessarily promote commensality.

Miriam said she eats breakfast and lunch at the office, with lunch being her main meal of the day. Like many other Google employees, she times her lunch to ensure she gets the food she wants—usually around noon. She mentioned that almost everyone eats lunch at twelve o'clock on the dot. It is not necessarily out of hunger (she often has breakfast around 9:30 a.m. and, generally, is not hungry again at 12 p.m.), but out of fear that, by 12:30 or 1 p.m., some of the best foods would be gone. So, she prefers forcing herself to eat early rather than missing out. Is this another strategy to get people to eat together? Given the amount of information Google has on its employees, it is likely aware of what, why, and when employees eat (Chance et al. 2016).

When I asked if she cooks at home, Miriam laughed and said, "No, not really at all. I often buy food but find that it goes off because I don't eat it." She lives alone, so her incentive to cook is low.

After lunch, I had a quick espresso from the coffee bar (which was excellent) and she showed me back out to the main building. We stood for a moment reflecting on the idea of working for a large company and the issues that technology has created in the workplace. Miriam was at once critical and realistic about her work but sparked some reflections about benefits and entitlement that I discuss further on. Back in the Google cafeteria, we said our goodbyes. She went back to work, and I sat down to write my notes.

Clearly, free food is not incentive enough for people to take a job. Consider restaurant workers, for example. They get free food, too, but surely do not take the job for that reason. Motivations are more nuanced and vary from person to person. However, once you start labelling free food as a perk rather than a reason sine qua non, the story changes. I turned to Quora, the Q&A website, to help find answers to the question "What is the best Google employee perk and why?" Most answers list food and drink above anything else. The frequency at which people answered that the best perk was the people, the business, and the technology is also high. As one respondent wrote, "Take these away, and no amount of food, gym, or shuttle buses can make up for it."

Alphabet's (the parent company of Google) Securities and Exchange Commission report from 2015 in the United States discusses recruitment and benefits as "risk factors" and I find it interesting that it has been included in this document.

While lengthy, and full of legal talk, they do, without mentioning free food directly, understand the efforts they have to make to keep talent. Free food is part of their corporate culture. They address the idea that teamwork is important but don't discuss directly how that is meant to be supported except to say that their culture "fosters" it. What they don't say is that their culture also fosters long hours, and that food (and other perks) are used as a way to help mitigate those hours.

In a list of perks that employees at Google have access to taken from the book *Work Rules!,* free food is listed at high cost to the company, no cost to the employee, and community and innovation are listed as benefits (Bock 2015). What about a full belly? Is that not a benefit for the employee? What about less stress in thinking about what to make for lunch at home and bring to work, or where to go out for lunch (which could easily fall into the efficiency category)? The rest alone would hardly justify the impact that a free food program such as Google's has on the employer's finances. It is clear that food is a form of value between company and employee.

Bock argues that nearly every perk they provide is for free or low cost. The main goal of which is to help create efficiency, community, or innovation. An important fact is that he here, again, mentions that the perks are not some "gilded cage, a trick designed to convince Googlers to work more or stick around longer. That fundamental tally misunderstands not just our motives, but also how work happens in companies like ours" (Bock 2015). Don't be evil, says Google, and it seems Bock is trying to back that up.

Often, food programs reflect the company vision or culture in itself. I found Google's food spaces to be extravagant. A similar feeling is echoed in Miriam's account of the overwhelming amount of information available to workers at Google (not to mention the amount of information that Google provides to internet users around the world). There is a lot of food, a lot of information, and a lot of work to do.

My conversation with Miriam and my introduction to free food at work both bring to mind Karen Ho's ethnography about finance workers in New York. Both groups are recruited from top universities, work long hours, and have food perks. In finance, there are two essential perks that reinforce the culture of hard work: dinner and a ride home (Ho 2009, 90). Giving employees the opportunity to order dinner on the company after 7 p.m. is essential in order for the company to keep employees at work longer. It is essential to the employees, too, since, given their long hours, they rarely make it to the grocery store. Employees might be able to expense meals from local restaurants, but at what rate do they become dependent on the service? Just like in the tech industry, some employees stay past 7 p.m., in order to have dinner (Ho 2009).

This is not so different from what Miriam told me about her own life: not going to the grocery store much and not cooking at home. Ho's account of the finance sectors shows that companies have been using food as an incentive to work longer since at least 1998 (and maybe before). We would like to think there are some key differences between finance and tech, and there are, but essentially both are using food to sustain a culture that demands long hours, or is an industry where there will always be those who feel the personal need or pressure to work longer, harder, faster.

Overall, my immersion in these food programs reminded me of one crucial thing: that the tech sector is not the only one to provide free staff meals. To really appreciate what it means to feed your staff and create a commensal, bonding atmosphere, it is worth taking a look at the restaurant industry.

The Family Meal

In the book *Around the Tuscan Table* Baldo, a member of a family in Tuscany, says that "eating together is the foundation of the family."[1] Restaurants have been feeding employees for decades and commonly call their meal a "family" meal. In America during the nineteenth century, many restaurant employees lived with the proprietors above or near the eatery. Beriss reports that after Hurricane Katrina ravaged New Orleans "eating in restaurants turned into one of the central ways the city's social fabric was to be rewoven" (Beriss et al. 2007, 2) showing that the city and the social lives of its residents revolve around eating out. All too aware that employees need sustenance to be productive, many restaurants have been offering at least a meal to their staff without being legally obliged to do so (Thring 2011). With this in mind, I visited a restaurant in London to gather some insight into how restaurants feed their employees and, hopefully, cast a light on some key aspects of food programs in tech companies, like commensality and conviviality. Here is how it went.

I arrived at the Clove Club, the one-Michelin-starred restaurant in Shoreditch, in East London—an area that is known for its hipster culture and trendy dining scene—at around 4 p.m. Rike, the business manager, gave me a quick tour of the open plan kitchen and dining room. Space matters in restaurants, not only for diners but for employees, too, she explained (a concept discussed in detail in a later chapter). At the Clove Club, the staff (or "family") meal is consumed in the dining room. Having a space to sit down and eat together is meaningful; it helps bring people together. But it is also a luxury that other restaurants, especially small ones, might not have. More often than not, staff get to eat a bowl of food while standing around in the kitchen—which, on many levels, is not exactly conducive to building a team.

I watched the dining room transform to host the family meal. Waiters took white, crisp tablecloths from a cupboard and laid them out on the tables, which had been pushed together to form a long one. Next, they arranged glassware and water bottles. Finally, they stacked napkins, utensils, and plates next to the food, which was ready to be served from large heating trays. There was a sweet smell of roasted pumpkin.

Rike handed me a plate and I filled it with an assortment of food: salad, roasted vegetables, quiche, and sausages. I took a seat. Everyone was eating quickly. I tried to take my time and ask a few questions, but after about fifteen minutes, I was left alone with Rike while everyone was standing up to go after their duties. "Dan, the chef, will come over for a chat when he has a chance, in a few minutes," someone said. As I was cleaning my own plate, I watched the dining room change into an elegant space, ready for the evening's service to begin.

The front of house staff paused to change into starched white shirts with grey linen aprons over the front. They moved swiftly, in step with each other like ballet dancers. The dirty tablecloths came off, piled in a bag with the napkins. Plates were stacked near the dishwasher along with the silverware and glasses, water bottles refilled and placed in the fridge. Then, the long table came apart and the chairs were re-arranged. Lights went down as candles were placed on the tables. The transformation was an amazing act to watch.

I was observing the barman arrange bottles and wash glasses when Dan, the chef, came over. We chatted for a few minutes about the importance of the staff meal and talked about who prepares it. "It's important that the food is of a good quality, and that it is filling and energetic, but not so heavy that it makes them feel groggy." The kitchen staff takes turns in cooking for everybody. Restaurant kitchens have a clear hierarchy, like the military, and building trust through cooking for each other is key. Moreover, in an industry in which staff turnover is sky-high, the family meal helps to create a sense of belonging. "It's important to get new people involved in the team," Dan said.

He also told me about their waste management and recycling policy, and how they repurpose leftovers or pieces of meat and fish that are not suited for the restaurant into the staff meal. Recycling is fine, but it is clear that the most important reason for feeding the restaurant staff is to ensure that they have enough energy to sustain their physical job. If the food is good, all the better.

Since the restaurant is closed on Sundays, most employees go for a drink on Saturday night to finish out the workweek. A sous chef told me that it is rare to have Sundays off in the restaurant industry. To him, it was a way for the company to show that they cared.

A number of cookbooks filled with restaurants' family meal recipes have hit the shelves proving the value that these meals have well beyond the enclosed world of professional kitchens. We have yet to see a cookbook on the food consumed in Google's offices.

One of the main aspects that set tech companies apart from restaurants is who prepares the food and where. In restaurants, the kitchen brigade take turns in preparing meals for the entire staff, in full sight of both back and front of the house. In tech companies, by contrast, service workers prepare all meals out of sight of the rest of the employees.

The divide between who prepares and who consumes the food is critical. Company B was well aware of the existing discrepancies between service and knowledge workers and made a few attempts to balance them. It tried, for example, to put in place a company-wide washing-up roster. Given the number of employees, the idea proved impractical. However, the divide in labor conditions remained an issue too great to ignore, particularly as it often led to a feeling of entitlement in knowledge workers. This was something the company strived to contain.

On the topic of having a separate cooking space, Elias writes about how thresholds of disgust have shifted and that "the distasteful" aspects of food preparation are removed from the sight of civilized society (Elias 1978, 121). This stance is particularly interesting when applied to a restaurant like the Clove Club, which has its kitchen in full view of the customers, and, too, when applied to tech offices, which, as Elias suggests, succeed in concealing all aspects of food preparation, including the cooks. This is reminiscent of the disconnect consumers experience when buying a packaged piece of meat: they see none of the behind-the-scenes, hence feeling detached from the food they consume.

At the Clove Club, the entire staff stopped their work to eat together, consistent with theories of commensality. "For at least the past three decades, the ideal in the United States and Western Europe has been for family members to come together for the evening meal" (Ochs and Shohet 2006, 37). Within social worlds, the family is the most fundamental, and perhaps the most common, commensal unit, followed by work groups (Sobal and Nelson 2003). Commensal units are groups of people who come together at a particular time and specific place to consume meals, snacks, and drinks together.

A number of postmodern, structural individualistic practices can, and do, invade people's ability to eat together. The fast pace of society, long work hours, and dietary individualism all contribute to what Fischler has called the "gastro-anomie" (Fischler 1979, 189). Food and dining can be, as it is easy to forget, inclusive and exclusive. It shows how society, to some extent, has shifted away from what was once considered an ideal meal, which is a meal eaten with others (Douglas 1972, Murcott 1982, Charles and Kerr 1986, Prättälä et al. 1993, Bell and Valentine 1997).

Several similarities exist between the family meal at the restaurants and the family meal at home. Both groups sit down to eat together; both groups are eating a meal prepared for them by one or more of them; both groups are expected to eat at (more or less) the same time. In this sense, the large body of work on the subject of the family meal at home becomes useful to analyze the meals that employees eat together (Dreyer and Dreyer 1973, Murcott 1982, Douglas 1999, Greenhill 2000, Ochs and Shohet 2006, Danesi 2017). Similarities aside, one difference jumps out: if the family meal at home is in decline, the family meal in restaurants remains constant.

Tech offices, on the other hand, are more varied spaces. I observed many different mealtimes, food prepared by a number of different people (rarely the same), and groups that did not always sit down to eat together. At Company A in London, drivers delivered meals at noon three days a week; employees ate when they wanted, sometimes at their desk and even as late as 4 p.m. At Company A in San Francisco, lunch was served from noon until around 1:30 p.m. Most employees ate toward the beginning of that time frame, many together, only a few at their desk. Company B's employees were fond of eating together and, for the most part, this is what I observed in London, San Francisco, and Dublin, where a large portion of each office stopped for lunch and gathered at long communal tables. This is the closest I found to the family meal at the Clove Club.

Before I left the Clove Club that evening, before the first guests arrived for their prepaid meal (they operate a ticketing system), I snapped a few photos and thought about the space—how the family meal here, while short, was meaningful and that the chef, Dan, understood the reasons why it was necessary. The added fact of preparing meals for your colleagues adds an even deeper dimension to their work, one that tech offices would struggle to imitate. This brings me back to the original research question about creating a space in which food helps to foster collaboration and teamwork in the tech office and how that plays out. What I discovered is that unlike the restaurant where cooperation is imperative, the tech office relies on a much looser idea of cooperation and teamwork because of the disconnected ways in which employees work and the lack of physical closeness to other colleagues. I guessed that if the higher-ups in tech companies could observe the Clove Club's family meal, they would probably be jealous.

The Food Culture of Company B

> If the number one thing you talk about your job is the free food and the ice cream bar, then there's something missing. (Katie, employee, Company B, London, in reference to a friend who works at Facebook.)

Company B's food program operates on a slightly different model and ethos than that of Google's. The company does not have any commercial kitchens inside offices. Instead, following a motto of promoting small-scale economic activity, it contracts small cafes and restaurants to cater for employees once a week.[2] Company B claims that this provides a direct economic link back to their community. On the other days, employees are encouraged to go out and spend their money in the neighborhood—as, again, this is in keeping with their corporate culture of supporting small-scale businesses.[3] Paolo Rossi, their former[4] global head of food, was quoted as saying:

> We want people to eat here and share food, but we also want people to get out and support local businesses and take a walk. We want to be porous to the community. And we want to foster a sense of gratitude and specialness instead of a sense of entitlement. (Simpson 2015)

Company B, in Paolo's words, is trying not to be an insular company, like Google, but to engage with surrounding communities. One way to achieve this is by locating offices in areas that have an active food scene, as opposed to having sprawling campuses miles away from a town center. As we will see, though, this is often easier said than done.

The first day I was at the Company B office in London, it was clear that they had a very different way of applying their food program from what I had seen at Google or the Clove Club. My liaison was Jennifer, an upfront and no-nonsense woman in her early thirties, originally from Australia. Her job title was "workplace operations specialist."[5] On her LinkedIn profile this is how she categorized her role at Company B:

> Creating a dynamic, safe, and enjoyable environment for all employees and visitors. Project management of internal operations, including vendor and stakeholder relationship management and implementation of data-driven processes

designed to increase efficacy. Ensuring our values are met and exceeded in daily life to assist our community.

She assigned me a desk with a view of the kitchen and gave me a tour of their new office. They had moved in two months prior; an artist was still finishing some of the murals on the walls. The office was bright with a lot of natural light. My notes refer to it as "warm and cocoon-like" and "very clean." It had a classic open office floor plan, no cubicles or personal offices (with the exception of the EMEA head, which I never met as she was constantly traveling). There were meeting rooms on the bottom floor, all with videoconference abilities. The kitchen area was closed off from the main office by a wall. Upstairs, a small kitchenette stocked a kettle, a coffee machine, and a few snacks.

The main kitchen had fresh fruit, several jars of nuts, oats, granola, cereals, dried fruit, multiple types of tea, a coffee machine, organic yogurt, fresh local milk delivered in glass bottles, large bulk bags of oats, snack bars, popcorn, and pita chips—all high-quality brands, mostly organic, focused on "healthy choices."

I found the gender-neutral bathrooms well stocked with all sorts of toiletries: feminine care products, organic hand soap, lotion, and items like earbuds, toothbrushes, and toothpaste. One bathroom had a shower with organic, locally sourced soap, shampoo, and conditioner. I noted also that the office itself had no smell, that there was no music playing (unlike at Company A), and that it was very quiet. Another point to note is that no one used their phones for calls—for the most part, any calls were taken by videoconference in one of the meeting rooms.

I found this fascinating and extraordinary—different from Miriam, at Google, who felt constantly connected to her work by her phone.

The kitchen was more of a preparation kitchen since, like I mentioned before, the food was prepared off-site and delivered. There was no oven or cooker to cook food. Claire was a part-time employee and responsible for setting the tables, getting the food put into serving trays, and managing some of the ordering and invoicing, especially the snacks from Ocado (an online grocery store popular in the United Kingdom). There was a second part-time employee who only arrived in the afternoon to help clean up the kitchen after lunch and tidy up the office in general. Both worked two to three days a week, with Jennifer as their supervisor. From my perspective, it seemed as if one job had been split among three people. It was hard to know what kept Jennifer seemingly so busy. It also echoed the cleaning woman at the Company A office across town. It became apparent the employees in these offices are used to being cleaned up after.

Figure 3.2.   Main dining area/prep kitchen at Company B, London

Of the thirty employees in the office, only two were men. This stands in contrast with most tech companies, which are heavily male-centric. Company B, on the other hand, has a near 50/50 split globally. I found their office in Dublin to be mostly women and, in San Francisco, a balanced mix.

While I was in the London office, Company B provided lunch on Tuesday and Thursday, as all Company B offices did. (That is not to say that employees were required to eat the Company B meals. Jennifer maintained a list of who was on holiday or out for a lunch meeting or did not want to eat what was on the menu that day.) On the remaining days, employees were encouraged (by the official food program policy) to go out; few did. Employees remembered their old office as having more dining options available close by than the new office, which was in the residential area. Almost every cafe or restaurant required a bus ride or a walk of at least fifteen minutes one way.

Luckily for them, lunches were plentiful and always resulted in a lot of leftovers. I saw a number of employees (including myself) take advantage of the leftovers on Monday, Wednesday, and Friday as opposed to leaving. Yet this goes against the strategic plan Company B has for their food program as Paolo Rossi says in an interview about their food program from 2015.

Rossi is very aware of the food perks provided by other tech companies, like Google, and he is committed to making sure that Company B carves a different path. At Google headquarters, employees have access to daily, on-site breakfast, lunch and dinner, but [Company B] made the conscious decision to serve food just twice a week. (Simpson 2015)

Eating leftovers is easier than going out, especially if choices are limited. When choosing a new office building, however, there seemed to be less thought put into its proximity to cafes and restaurants than its ability to function as an office space and its cost. Access and ease are not the only reasons why employees do not go out much. Work, too, plays an important role. When asked if they feel overworked, no one said yes, at least not openly. Some of the challenges of working for a multinational company (where your direct supervisor might be in Brooklyn, the global headquarters) are that you might need to be available for an online meeting at times that are less than convenient. Work teams are spread out. It is a global business. This is something that Company B, Google, and Company A, where employees work across different time zones, all share and it can be daunting for some employees to manage.

Elizabeth Keating in her book *Words Matter: Communicating Effectively in the New Global Office* picks up this point and says that "the ability to project ourselves into the 'virtual' intercultural space of the global office involves a tremendous loss of cultural, environmental, and nonverbal context. This affects the resources that people have for building common understanding. As a result, the ways people typically do language actions sometimes don't work right" (Keating and Jarvenpaa 2016, 72). Trying to design products, apps, websites, and so forth, with colleagues on different continents is challenging.[6]

On Tuesdays and Thursdays at 1 p.m. the lunch bell would ring, and Clair would call out "lunch." Employees stopped what they were doing and lined up in the kitchen to eat together, like a family meal at a restaurant. Like the Clove Club's staff, Company B's employees ate quickly. I did not observe them taking their entire lunch hour—the average was thirty minutes.

Ringing the lunch bell is an important ritual for Company B and it reminded me of school. On occasion, someone might start eating later than the rest, but I never observed anyone taking a plate of food back to their desk—a startling fact! Startling because it happened in other offices (like Company A, London) more than I thought it would.

The food served at Company B is, for lack of a better word, healthy. I ate a lot of salads. Jennifer told me that they tried to eat less meat and carbs and more vegetarian and vegetable-focused meals. It was not a 100 percent vegetarian office, but many appreciated the healthy-leaning nature of the food. Jennifer was very open to suggestions—each day after lunch they were encouraged to leave their personal feedback about the meal, helping her and Clair judge which suppliers to continue to work with and what foods to

Figure 3.3.   A few of the meals I ate at the Company B office, London. Note the use of real cutlery, plates, and glasses—all reusable.

choose. No one badmouthed the food program—negative comments were rare.

Employees were generous with their thoughts about lunch. Francesca, an employee from Italy, told me about the transition from the older (more "unhealthy") meals to the current model, which reflected a more balanced, modern way to eat. She was one of a handful of workers who started in the smaller Dublin office. There, she said, lunches felt more "unhealthy": chips, pizza, and burgers were served frequently. Things improved with the arrival of an office manager, but Francesca still found meals to be starch heavy. "It's hard to focus in the afternoon after a lunch with a lot of potatoes," she said. The meals now are more in line with California Cuisine.

Potatoes or not, they were expensive lunches. With a budget of around £14 per person, per lunch, this office had one of the highest food expenditures I encountered. How can a company justify such a cost? Is it team building or is the company reaping rewards—like enhanced team performance—through the mundane but powerful act of eating (Kniffin et al. 2015, 281)? It is a good question and during the research I was not privy to any internal documents that justified this cost, only to later understand that Jennifer was given a budget which she could use as she saw fit. In the end, she didn't have to justify the £14 lunch, but only the overall monthly expenditures.

Collaboration

These are not basic ideas, but instead implicit social theories about the power of food. In many articles these social theories seem assumed, untested, and unproved. Was increased productivity confirmed through my research? Not entirely. Productivity is an elusive concept, one that has proven difficult to measure with qualitative methods. One employee explained that his commitment to productivity is that he tries to get his inbox to zero each day, or at least he tries not to leave if he knows that he has an unfinished task that will block someone else's ability to complete their work for that day. But how do employees arrive at the appropriate amount of work to do without a formal review process? When I asked about the link between productivity and free food, there was no consensus. A few mentioned that lighter foods like salads make them feel more productive in the afternoons, but a *feeling* of productivity is not the reality of productivity. A few alluded to the fact that it saves them time—they don't have to consider what to bring for lunch or where to go—but time savings do not equal productivity.

Another inherent mandate in the tech industry is collaboration. Companies realize its importance in the success of the business (Chen et al. 1998, 285). Every job advertisement states that the prospective employee should be willing to collaborate.

> Did we mention collaborative? We're a close family, and this role will work across many functions, and we need someone who is comfortable department surfing. (Company A job advertisement excerpt)

Derek, a product manager, expressed his thoughts about this over lunch one day, admitting that "employees who can't work as part of a team or collaboratively don't last long." It goes hand in hand with a workplace social order that prioritizes decentralized responsibility—when something goes wrong it is a team problem, not an individual problem. This style of working can make it difficult for any one employee to show the work they have done and prove themselves as individuals. But does free food contribute to more collaboration? Business academics claim that less time spent going off-site for food equals more time to collaborate, but what I assert is that collaboration happens anyway; it is ingrained in the workplace culture of the industry (Kniffin et al. 2015). It can't be taken for granted, you have to make it possible and encourage it.

In the conversation with Derek, he told me that "employees are adaptable. They have adapted to free food and would adapt to not having it." That is to say that it wouldn't necessarily change the ways in which they work. You would have employees leaving during lunch to get food, but the pressure of the job that keeps them from taking an entire lunch hour would, most likely, remain. So how can we claim that free food makes employees more productive or more collaborative? We can't. Those are broad claims that have little or no basis in what actually happens in different offices. What happens, in my experience, is employees collaborate anyway and are as productive as they need to be, and free food is not really included in these considerations. It begs the question of, are incentives, like free food, necessary for collaboration and productivity? No, they are not.

These are not new ideas; most companies who provide meals understand these basics. In Laszlo Bock's book about the corporate culture of Google he tells us that the programs are there to achieve three goals "efficiency, community and innovation" but also to relieve hard working employees from "time-consuming, mundane, chores." (Bock 2015, 275)

These carefully orchestrated programs, in short, are in place to reduce life's encumbrances. This is true in each example—Company B, Company A, and Google. To be fair, many of the perks Bock discusses come at little or no cost to the company. Food, on the other hand, costs something, but it is also one of the most visible signs of care. These workers are expected to work intensively, and employers support them by delivering care, in various forms (English-Lueck and Avery 2017).

What does it mean to provide so much care for employees? Does the care of employees create a sense of loyalty to the company? When asked this question, employees at Company B were unsure, but when pressed to think about previous jobs without free food or future jobs without free food, they realized that it would be a very hard transition. This kind of loyalty might increase retention, but free food and job satisfaction are still difficult to link. English-Lueck makes the connection and says that "care also amplifies productivity and cements loyalty, however, ephemeral, to the employer" (English-Lueck and Avery 2017, 41). I believe that employees would continue to work long hours, change jobs, and be unhappy no matter whether they got free food or not. The financial industry is a prime example of this (Ho 2009).

This brings me to an essential finding in my research. Free food, it turns out, is not an optional perk for tech companies. It is a requirement. These programs and perks are creating a new workplace model that benefits the employees' well-being and, at the same time, an emerging class of workers whose lives are being more actively managed by their employers. These companies are creating a strong sense of identity, loyalty, and continuity through food. The tech industry changes rapidly but free meals can and do remain constant.

What makes Company B's program stand out, to me, is that it seems they have thought about what they want out of the program, what employees want, and what the community around the offices want—and they have attempted to address those. The company wants a food program that supports its mission statement and values, employees want to feel taken care of and valued, and the surrounding community doesn't want to lose out on the lunchtime crowd of hungry office workers. Paolo was instrumental in bringing these three forces together with his singular vision for what the food program is and can become. Paolo was also very aware of the power of entitlement.

Peapod, an online delivery service, revealed that two-thirds of workers, especially millennials, were "extremely or very happy" if given free snacks, and they "looked for such benefits in job-hunting" (Malcolm 2015). What happens, then, when entitlement to these perks creeps into the workplace? Sheryl, a senior international strategy, and operations manager at Company B in London, told me:

> Coming from a background working in startups, snacks were a big part of our office environment—I mean, we placed an order online from Sainsbury's each week and we could all make suggestions on what to get. But I wouldn't take a job based on snacks or free food—but the snacks here are much better. I mean, you can tell they try.

From Perks to Entitlement

Where do you want to eat lunch? In Central London, this simple question can produce great anxiety. "There are more than 100 places to get lunch within a 10–15-minute walk," I wrote in my field notes. One day, while visiting Company A's office in London, I tried to count them. Soon enough, I realized that it was going to be an arduous task. Like Company B's, the majority of Company A's employees ate the free lunch they were given twice a week. Unlike Company B's, they had lot of options to choose from on alternate days. I asked Christopher about this one day.

Christopher was in his late sixties. He was tall and lanky with a thick bob of white hair. He had a young child at home and commuted from a small village near Bristol, a trip that takes the better part of two hours. He worked from home two days a week. He was the sole member of the legal team in the London office; his supervisor was in San Francisco. He started his job a few months before I arrived. One day, we had a long conversation about labor and his role at Company A. Talking about how work has changed over the past thirty years, he remembered being able to go on vacation without ever hearing from the business, or to go home in the evening and enjoy time with his family, no mobile phone to keep him company. Still, he liked the free lunches, and confessed that it was the first time he had been given lunch at work. He recalled his student years in London when meal options were limited to pubs and the occasional sandwich shop. "The number of choices you have now is staggering," he said. He rarely ate any snacks, drank the bare minimum of coffee and tea, and in general seemed to be one of the most satisfied employees in the office.

Several things stood out about Christopher. For one, he took his entire lunch hour—a rarity in this like in many offices—and went for a walk—and then, he ate alone at his desk instead of eating with others. When I asked him about this, he said it was the only time he had to read the news or check his personal email. Unlike younger employees, who would not think twice about reading the news or checking their personal email throughout the workday, Christopher insisted on doing these things "off the clock" during his lunch. I found this telling, not just of his generation, but of the generation that makes up most of the tech industry these days. He gave his full attention to the work he was doing.

Martin earned his PhD in computer sciences from Stanford. He was one of the older employees at Company B's office in San Francisco, nine years on the job. Asian American, with a very Northern California attitude about him (casual yet confident), Martin's presence in the office was that of a supportive and wise uncle. With a long career in the Bay Area, he had a lot of knowledge to share. One of Martin's first jobs was at Yahoo, where he says the only food perk was free coffee. His attitude toward food is intriguing. In our interview, he said that "the dollar investment [for food] is small compared to the impression that it makes on the employee" and that "the impression that food has on employees is much higher than if the company just gave them a check for some odd amount at the end of the year—the impression is important. Employees talk about it—newspapers write about it." He continued:

> Food plays into the younger employee population. They are the ones doing most of the "backbreaking" work—fresh out of school, knowing the latest things about the industry. They have no family or kids, generally, and food plays directly into this. The role of food changes as the company ages. It starts with "Let's keep you on campus as long as possible" and, as employees age and the company matures, it moves towards "It's really convenient to not have to think about lunch and food." You don't have to carry a lunch. Benefits turn toward things like, "Do you offer childcare?"

The changing nature of how employees perceive the perks shows that as employees age, as their life experiences shift, as they become more "adult"; they soon realize that free food isn't just a meal—some do see free food as a means of control—especially if you look at message boards such as Reddit. Most employee experiences though, are not negative. Beyond a critical error in judgment by some to see free food and perks as merely a means of control and power domination, there are instances where free food is used as a way to create community through the act of eating together; this could be seen as exploitative and, in some ways, hides the true nature of the gift.

When I ask employees if they would be willing to replace free food for more money, the answers tended to veer towards the idea of "how much"— but more often than not, what came up was that there was a value to having food provided for you in that it saved you time and money. Overall, I think that each employee found it hard to quantify just how much money the free food was worth, because it was not just about the cost of the food itself, but the added value of time, energy, and thinking about what, when, and where to eat. These are personal and hard to measure.

The hidden side of these food gifts is that it helps to create community. Money, instead, would be counter-intuitive to the idea that eating together helps build a cohesive work unit, and if the company can encourage that, then all the better for them. The other side of this argument, though, is just how much community is created in the lunchroom and does community trump work priorities and busyness?

This goes hand in hand with another observation I made, that employees take extra snacks for the weekend. As reported, this goes against what Charlotte, the food program manager at Company A in San Francisco, would like to happen, but there are not set in stone rules against it. This plays on the idea first introduced by Sahlins that you can't profit from the gift or you are destroying the meaning of the gift (Sahlins 1974, 161). The companies here want the food to be marked as a gift rather than as compensation by other means. Another example from the field is the account of the CEO of Company B taking questions about the food program and specific products like kombucha—these are trivial questions, yes, but also you're not supposed to discuss the nature and value of the gifts.

Charlie Ayers, Google's first chef, gave some of the best accounts of free food in Silicon Valley, especially regarding the beginning of the food program at Google and the influence it had on the industry at large. He cashed out of the company in 2005 to run his own restaurants. On the podcast Internet History (2017), he declared that employees can

> exchange thoughts and ideas over breaking bread. No one was bringing different groups together over food like Google. The soup and bread areas were a place

they liked to gather in the afternoon when they were trying to figure something
out. It had a very university feel to it. [Food became] a recruiting tool so people
understood this is how you're going to be treated and fed. [Employees] loved
cereal and food that didn't need anything done to it. [Google's cafe] became a
sought-out place to eat that there was no reservation for.

Charlie understood the value that a meal like this could bring—he understood
the ways in which eating together help with morale and team building. He
also realized that by creating a place that was coveted, they had an angle for
recruitment—they actively promoted the value of the gifts. I don't take the
view of Sahlins, though, that they destroyed its meaning. They actually gave
food meaning on purpose—they elevated it to mean something more: they
talked about it as something desirable, difficult to obtain, necessary.

At the beginning, free food was very much a perk and, as Charlie says, a
recruiting tool. Google was offering something no one else was. Now, things
are different. Most tech companies have their own food programs because
none of them want to be the outsider. So, really, the question a prospective
employee will ask these tech companies now is not "Do you offer food?" It's
more along the lines of "What kind of food do you offer, and how much?"

One of the first interviews I conducted was with Mike, Company A's UK
director. He shared some thoughts with me about food at his company and
in the tech industry in general. Mike is in his late forties, tall and lanky with
short cropped blonde hair. He has a small protruding belly and tired eyes. He
commutes from the countryside four days a week and has two small children
at home. Some of the highlights of our conversations are

> Company A is an office-based culture and people should be in the office to build
> the office community. There are four functions in this office and there is always
> food in mind. Free food is now a minimum requirement for tech offices—this
> came from San Francisco and the entitlement that has been created by the large
> companies is a "scary *enfant terrible*." There is a certain set of basic benefits
> that are required now, and food is one of them. All of the companies that started
> in California and San Francisco now have to figure out how to do this in other
> countries. Food culture in San Francisco is inherently healthier. Entitlement is
> rampant in the tech industry. (Mike, UK/Ireland manager, Company A)

These comments came straight from the top, from someone that had worked
at Google for several years before joining Company A. I was impressed by
his frankness, and his ability to see some of the problems. Considered with
Martin's account, it is fairly clear that, yes, entitlement does exist. Martin's
thoughts on this matter came toward the end of his interview when I asked
him about the cuts that were taking place to Company B's food program.
Here is the transcript:

Int: What do you think of the food program being cut in half? What's your general impression? Expected, unexpected? I know there are a lot of changes happening in the company at the moment.

M: Oh boy. It's hard to answer that question, divorced of the context that happened at the moment. It kind of felt like death by a thousand paper cuts. Like, every day there's a little bit of bad news. It really sucks. It's a terrible signal to send [to employees]. The food really makes an impression upon people, so I felt like, having said that, there was an office hours back when [the former CEO] was still here, a few months ago, and do you know how our office hours are run here? I guess you wouldn't have been allowed to see it, probably.

Int: You mean the company-wide meetings? They mentioned it but I haven't taken part in one.

M: I think we're officially not meant to have guests at them. But anyway, Robin started this tradition where once a week it was just an open forum. He would be there, and you could come in person and ask questions, or you could go online if you're remote like us and ask questions and they would be asked for you. It was a free for all; you could ask whatever you wanted to ask.

Int: Anonymous?

M: It was anonymous. Then they got rid of those questions. So, a few months back, like six or seven months back probably, it was just cringeworthy. A number of the questions had to do with the meals, the timing of lunch, reheating food, breakfast, I think that by the fifth question or something Robin was about to blow his top and he's like, you people need to think about—you are talking with the CEO, you need to think, "This is my opportunity to ask a question. What am I going to use that time for?" We're not a huge company, but still. It was really telling. Like I and a lot of people that left that office hours were like, "Wow, people here are really spoiled." And hand in hand with that whole theme of trying to build up accountability in the company, there's this theme; some of these people don't really know what the real world's like and people are pretty spoiled here, so food going away had the feeling like those people are just going to lose their tops.

Int: Do you think some will flee?

M: People already are for other reasons, but yeah, yeah.

Jennifer at Company B in London echoed Martin's thoughts about entitlement, especially about the question-and-answer session with the CEO.

Yeah, it can get ridiculous sometimes. I mean, when we had the question and answer times with Robin [the CEO], people were asking things like "When is the kombucha on level nine going to be refilled?" As if he would know the answer to that. They just weren't taking it seriously. It was really a waste of everyone's time.

Entitlement is rampant in the tech industry; we hear from two long-term employees in two different cities and in two different companies. How did it get to this? Because the companies are full of people who do not know what the "real world is like." Employees demand (or ask?) to be treated like others in the industry. This situation also reinforces the idea, from English-Lueck, of moving from one kind of university-style support system to another. Younger employees right out of college are fresh faces ready to work long hours, and if you can blanket their transition by providing free food, all the better.

Talking about entitlement veers easily into pop-psychology. Martin and Jennifer think that entitlement exists but when they discuss it, it seems like it doesn't apply to them. It does. They are just as entitled as any other employee. But to be allowed to participate in the society of entitlement, you have to agree to be "ripped off" (Appleyard 2013). They are being ripped off and more time is spent engaged in work (or at the office) than in the past. They are compensated well, overall—the basic incomes of those working in San Francisco are high, even if the cost of living there is equally as high. This position of relative wealth in society can lead to a feeling of entitlement, and it does and employees experience this just walking down the street to the front door of the office, again, intensifying the divide. We only need to look at the ways in which many CEOs of tech companies act out of irreverence for rules, laws, and regulations—they are above them (Isaac 2017, Pao 2018, Swisher 2018)!

Ho discusses the recruitment of new college graduates at length in her book, and although her research is in finance, her comments apply to tech companies too. Are straight-out-of-college hires connected to a feeling of entitlement? Hard to tell. But there are definitely a few employees who think that younger recruits are falling victim to a hand-holding type of job. From Ho's book,

> The point is to create a post college atmosphere where, within days of beginning work, analysts and associates begin to "live" there, comparing notes about who is staying the latest and "getting slammed" the most, not to mention participating in the makeshift Nerf football game at 1 a.m. (Ho 2009, 90)

If perks have the drawback of making people blasé and entitled, what value do they actually have? And where does all this entitlement lead? According to Martin, it leads to awkward conversations with CEOs. It leads to arguments over coffee (which is discussed at length later), and to food program managers needing to understand a range of dietary restrictions in order to perform their duties and provide the requisite care. My study of free food in the tech industry, I realized, was an ethnography on the everyday life of entitlement, the micro-interactions that make privilege seem normal and expected.

Melissa Salazar tells us that American adults can easily and quickly recall the school lunches and school cafeterias of their childhoods. She suggests this is a direct result of the power that these meals and spaces have (Salazar 2007, 154). Many of the tech offices have eating spaces that feel a lot like a school cafeteria. Students, like employees, eat in large, sometimes crowded, rooms under the "watchful eyes" of others. Salazar's work deals with Mexican immigrants' experiences in trying to fit in both "with their food habits and where to sit."

Showcasing the pressure that eating together can cause, tech companies are taking a risk in creating divisions as much as cohesion. Commensality is a risk that companies assume translates into an enhanced community. Considering my own experience in school and in these companies, the comparison is real. There was a feeling of unease in not knowing where to sit or with whom. In a previous job, the lunchroom was divided into culture groups—the Indians would eat together and more often than not would bring in food to share amongst themselves. The Italians ate the latest and complained about the bad pasta. The English ate at random times, were more likely to sit alone, and would watch TV or use their mobile phones. In Company B and Company A, work groups were more likely to eat together—the sales team, marketing and communication, engineering, product. What physical divisions existed in the offices were enhanced in the lunchroom.

At Company B and Company A, eating alone at your desk was a clear sign that you didn't want to be bothered. There is a real problem here between commensality and excluding people. What I observed is that it is personal. The idea of the lunch break is that it is your time to do with what you want—by forcing commensality you take away the idea of lunch as a break from work. Christopher's account is a perfect example of this. To him, it was a break from work entirely and that not only meant his work email, but his colleagues as well.

The number of food programs like these has reduced the more traditional packed lunch, which seems to offer the most choice for everyone. From my own personal history, I remember my father and grandfather packing their own lunches each day for work in matching lunchboxes (usually a sandwich or some leftovers). Working long shifts in an oil refinery, they both relied on those meals. When asked about the lunch breaks, my dad recounted how those were clear breaks in their workday when they would eat together with a group of colleagues, but each with their own packed lunch from home. Both my grandmother and mother worked and so were relieved, for the most part, from the chore of preparing lunches for the men. This kind of "hidden" food preparation is common also in the tech industry, where some food is prepared off-site and catered into the offices. This is reminiscent of the idea presented by Trubek of the "invisible army" and that the location of paid cooks has changed over the course of history in the United States (Trubek 2017, 72). While she considers these through a historical class structure, what I observed in these offices is that the food is either being prepared by restaurants or by professional catering staff. The two I encountered at Company A in San Francisco were both white males in their late twenties.

Changes in provisioning and domestic labor are also part of the shift away from packed lunches. There are occupations where leaving isn't an option (e.g., a refinery or a hospital). There are now less strict codes regarding women who pack lunches for men—mealtimes have shifted and been altered, and people eat when they want. Cafes have stepped in to take the place of the packed lunch because it's easier and quicker. Those who do take their own food (like I used to do in nearly every job I've had) are looked at with suspicion. So, it sets that group apart. Even if space is available to eat together, showing up with a packed meal from home gives the impression that the food that you're given isn't good enough. Ho says bringing your own lunch was a sign of being frugal—or that you were worried about money—something that only those working in the "back office" did (who I assume, get paid less than those in the "front office") (Ho 2009, 121). In the tech industry lunch seems to be linked to ideas of commitment; bringing your own lunch might be a sign of having more free time than others, going out to get your lunch comes in a close second, and finally, eating at work, as everyone else does, shows commitment—eating at your desk, even more. Of note, though, is that one employee at Company B in San Francisco, Devon, mentioned in an interview something close to the lunch discussion in Ho's book.

Devon: I wish I could take my entire lunch hour, you know. No one tells you that you can't, but really, *you can't.*

Int: So, you get a full hour, but no one takes it—and the office is so small, that if you do take it, then your colleagues know?

Devon: Exactly. Some days, you know, I'd just like to be able to get outside, go for a walk, get some fresh air.

Ho's discussion of the social class associated with a packed lunch doesn't fit into the tech industry framework entirely, though there is a division between engineers (who typically get paid more) and other employees whose salaries might be slightly lower. In my observations, this did not translate into a group who brought their lunch and a group that did not—because most tech companies treat all employees the same in terms of perks. Everyone has access to the same free food in the office.

Going back to Martin and Mike's thoughts on entitlement—particularly, to Mike's comments about how there now must be a given set of benefits, and to Martin's comments about asking the CEO questions about lunch—it is clear that the tech industry has created a problem. How do you rectify needing to offer free food in order to attract the best employees and, at the same time, teach employees the value of the free food they are eating? It is a difficult balance.

Neither Mike nor Martin brought their lunches. Both assumed their ritualistic positions in the office, and both ate the lunches that were provided—as if on cue. Mike, on one hand, did like to complain about the vegetarian options and would make a small fuss if he had to go out to get something "better or more filling" as he would put it. Martin, on the other hand, seemed to have a very accepting point of view toward the food offered. Maybe it was because of his long tenure in the industry or maybe he just wasn't that picky—I like to think that it's partially both.

Employees might appreciate the food available in the office more when they got less of it or when they were charged for it. Either could help curb the sense of entitlement, but it would not help on the recruitment and retention fronts. Overall, the employees in the London offices seemed to appreciate free food more than those in San Francisco, but I think this came down to the fact that free food is less common in offices in London than in San Francisco.

"Enjoy it while you can, for you never know when they'll take it away," goes the adage. During my time at Company B, the company had to slash their food program in half. When companies are required to cut costs and reduce budgets, food is often the first to be reduced, even though it is an entrenched expectation. It is not guaranteed in contracts; it is an assumed benefit. And this is because food programs, though beneficial to both companies and employees, do not generate any revenue. I'll pick this up in the next chapter, where I discuss food programs and budgets, the issue with Company A providing dinner in San Francisco, and the delicate balance that the food program managers must have between keeping their budget in line and keeping employees fed (and happy).

NOTES

1. See Counihan (2004).

2. When I first started my fieldwork with Company B, the company offered lunch twice a week on Tuesday and Thursday. After a series of company-wide layoffs and cutbacks, the company now only provides lunch once a week.

3. All of this has, of course, been challenged during the pandemic. While employees are at home, they are left to feed themselves, and that might be from local cafes or restaurants providing delivery or takeout.

4. Paolo was one of the employees made redundant during Company B's restructuring in 2017.

5. Jennifer's job was one of the positions that was cut during the second round of layoffs. That being said, it was challenging to keep track of her from an ethnographic standpoint. Digital platforms like LinkedIn proved useful, only to a point.

6. One can see how this would be even more the case during the pandemic.

Chapter Four

Finance and the Value of Snacks

FOOD IS THE FIRST TO GO

Workdays in tech offices can be long. Employers know that if you plan on keeping people away from the things they love for so long (family, pets, sunlight, friends) then they need something in return, usually food. From the last chapter, we know that food is ubiquitous in the tech industry but not guaranteed. Contracts do not promise it. This makes it an easy target when finances turn sour. You can see the rise and fall of a tech company in its changing food program.

Charlotte was the workplace specialist at Company A in San Francisco and my liaison. She was a bright, mid-twenties Asian American. Tall and slim, she wore her hair straight to her shoulders. Her desk was elevated, with a full view of the kitchen and eating space. She was perched, able to observe the dining, snack, and drinks areas. Charlotte was responsible for managing a large food budget for the office, which included breakfast, lunch, snacks, and dinners—even the rare catered executive meeting. Originally from Pennsylvania, she had a focused and rational way of speaking. She was down to earth, sensible, and dedicated. She was always completely attentive and rarely glanced at her phone and our conversations went uninterrupted—a rarity.

She was the first person to tell me that food was the first to go. This answers the question of what a company cuts back on first when finances are tight. Charlotte said:

> The facilities department just spends money. We don't generate anything. When I started here, about a year ago, not long after we started to do some drastic cuts. When we started those, it was requested for me to be discreet about it. But people noticed. It was really uncomfortable for me to keep it to myself and

have to defend it—and not be transparent about why, but kind of beat around the bush. I still think it is so generous and a bit unnecessary, to be honest. If I had it my way, we'd cut food on Friday all together and have a really strong Monday to Thursday game.

Free food is precious to employees. Charlotte reported that Company A employees routinely grumbled about a lack of choices, even with over sixty different snacks available in the office. Could it be that an overabundance of good food is a source of anxiety (Konnikova 2014)? It seems that it can, at least according to psychologists who study anxiety and choices (Schwartz 2005, Thaler and Sunstein 2009, Iyengar 2010, Scheibehenne et al. 2010). I tested this firsthand. Presented, as I was, with the same number of snacks, drinks, and food offered to real employees, I found that I became worried about which to choose. The offices with more food and snacks were even more daunting. Choice overload! Which snack should I pick? Would it keep me full enough? Would taking more than one drink cause employees to think I am greedy? If I pile my plate full of all the foods available at lunch, what would Charlotte think? That I am just a greedy researcher who chose to study these companies for the free meals? Charlotte had a lot of thoughts about snacks and especially about employees taking them home with them, which isn't banned, but, as she says, "I'm personally not stoked when someone grabs like eight bags of chips and throws them in their bag for the weekend."

I have to admit that having access to a large amount of free food at Company A meant that I had to practice my own form of temperance, of not eating too much. It was helpful, from the perspective of someone on a budget to have access to so much, but it also produced anxiety over choice that I did not experience at Company B, where there was no choice. I can say the same about the few lunches I ate at Google; I was overwhelmed with choice. With so many choices at hand, why did employees still complain about what they did not have? It is the difference between anxiety (of choice) and entitlement. People who feel comfortable with their privileges, who can navigate between them with no anxiety and even take them for granted, seemed to be the norm. I was not used to the access; I was not used to the privileges of being in the company. And I admit that this was a big learning curve for me—to not experience a personal sense of guilt for taking drinks, food, or coffee. Yet, I didn't speak with any employees who seemed to share this sentiment of guilt. In fact, several employees reported to me that they feel like they can "work it off." Their response to free food is to work longer and take shorter lunch breaks.

Feelings of guilt can also be associated with theories that surround gifting culture and exchange in general. I felt guilty taking the free food because I wasn't giving the company anything back in return—I wasn't working it off.

I was a "moocher"; I was freeloading off them. Some might have seen it this way, and it's true that I haven't given anything back to the companies (yet), but the point is that guilt in relation to gifting is about power. They had the power to strip me of my access to the office, the food, and the employees at any time, for any reason. My feelings of guilt played into this power they had by not wanting to be seen as someone who was just taking all I could from the basket of free food, and instead, playing a role or a part in the game. There was never any indication, from anyone, that I was a freeloader and just in it for the free food—never an indication that my presence was unwelcome. But that didn't change the fact that if I took one extra handful of almonds or drank one too many expensive smoothies, that I felt like someone was watching or judging me.[1]

FINANCIAL HEALTH AND THE PROBLEM WITH DINNER

It was close to noon on a Thursday and the dining area was starting to fill up at Company A's office in San Francisco. Employees come in groups, waves of workers in about ten-to-fifteen-minute shifts. It took most employees about thirty minutes to eat, judging by my watch. Some lingered longer in what appeared to be meetings more than lunch breaks—notebooks were out, and many employees arrived at lunch with their MacBook Airs, which some used as food trays.

After the initial hustle and bustle calmed down a bit, I got in line, chose some salad, bread, a few pieces of cheese, and a can of lemon LaCroix, and took a seat at a large square table with just two other guys sitting at it. I was within earshot, yet not close enough to feel like I was intruding. No one says hello. I sit down and listen.

> *Guy one:* My friend over at Company XYZ told me they are getting rid of free breakfasts.
>
> *Guy two:* Oh yeah?
>
> *Guy one:* Yeah, he's looking around for a new position if you hear of anything.

The quality and quantity of food available inside tech companies acts as a non-official indicator for the financial health of the company. Charlotte's comment about needing to keep cuts to the food program quiet would seem to confirm this; employees take cuts to the food program as a signal, a sign that something is amiss. This is an important insight in that it shows the importance that food has to employees and echoes Martin's comments on the perception that free food has. After overhearing this conversation, I realized that this was even true at Company B, where I heard about some employees looking for new jobs after the food program was cut in half. But this goes against what the very open nature that these companies claim to have toward diffusing information to employees. If employees are taking cues about how well the company is performing from the quantity or quality of the food choices, then there has been a severe communication problem. Company A, because it is a private company, does not have to disclose financial data to the public, so it is more difficult for employees there to understand how the company is performing than at Company B, which is public. Their stock price, financial records, and yearly earnings are all public—employees can use that information to gauge how well the company is doing but I doubt that many do.

Employees are acutely aware of changes in the food program. Charlotte, at Company A in San Francisco, sent out notices about any snacks or drinks that were out of stock, along with a weekly food menu. Kim had a similar email she sent out each week even if she planned meals a month in advance. Company B did the same by providing an online calendar of what was planned for lunches and asked employees to mark in advance if they were in the office for lunch that day or not.

All three women's jobs required them to react to budget changes. Kim mentioned that when the organization added a staff member, there was not necessarily more money put into her food budget. Jennifer had to not only manage a budget but also research each vendor to make sure it aligned with Company B's philosophy and vision for its food program. Charlotte's budget was even more complex due to the number of meals the company served, which included dinner.

Company A's San Francisco office was the only one of my primary field sites that provided dinner for employees. Dinners were controversial for several reasons. First of all, they were not well attended. The evenings I stayed for dinner it felt lonely, as most of the employees had already left. The office was eerily quiet. Second, dinner was an expense that, in Charlotte's view, was not performing, due to the lack of participation and so when faced with a reduction in her budget, she tried to cut it. In considering the research question, it doesn't seem to support teamwork and cooperation because it is so underutilized.

In reaction to her proposed cut, the engineering manager spoke up. As she tells it, he called the dinners the "engineering dinners" since mostly engineers stayed to eat them (I can confirm this). Charlotte pushed back, saying that "dinners were expensive and not many employees took part in them—engineers were only a fraction of the overall employee count." But he countered, saying that it was "a bonding opportunity for his team."

Eventually, Charlotte had to give in to his demands and keep dinner, cutting back elsewhere to accommodate the expense. The decision was not hers alone to make and required a number of conversations, as she says, with her direct manager and higher-ups. This highlights an important part of the Company A office and the tech industry overall; engineers are the stars.

Corporate care of employees was originally created for engineers and their managers, who were also engineers (English-Lueck and Avery 2017, 43). From my interviews, I know they can and do demand certain products (especially snacks) and are empowered to this elevated status by the greater tech community—they carry a lot of food influence. They command good salaries and are in high demand. They are the employees that companies fight for—the ones who might choose a job based on food. So, is it any surprise that Company A kept dinner?

The conversation about dinner made me wonder why I observed engineers starting later than other groups. They were never the first in the office and were usually the last to go home. Why were they eating dinner when others were not? There are many theories, or should I say, rumors about engineers being lazy, wanting to sleep in, staying up all night playing video games. It might be true for some, but definitely not all. I wanted to get to the bottom of this at Company A.

What I discovered was a connection between dinner and the actual work of an engineer. This was not a bonding opportunity for the team as stated by the engineering manager. Engineering is essentially writing code for long periods of time, which is mentally taxing—akin to translation. It requires uninterrupted focus in an environment free from distractions. The open office floor plans that these companies have adopted are not conducive to this kind of work. In fact, not only did engineers talk about the noise levels in the open offices, but employees from other departments did too (Kaufman 2014, Konnikova 2014).

I spoke to a number of engineers while in the office, but Kenny provided the most concrete information. First, he told me that "many of them are actually night owls." But, more importantly, "they tend to work late because, after around 5 pm, the office gets rather quiet because most employees are going home or at least, most of the phone calls and noise has calmed down. There are no meetings, the phones stop ringing, and the music is shut off. It is distraction free—perfect for writing code."

Dinner plays directly into these work habits, and it is the main reason that the engineering manager fought to keep it. Engineers eat dinner because they work late, and they work late because during the day the office is busy, loud, and distracting. So why not just give engineers their own offices or space to work in? It seems like a simple idea that would allow them to cut dinners.

The idealized benefits of building community through an open office floor plan seem to disguise the negative effects of an open office plan on actually doing work.

In line with this, I discovered that, in some offices, employees would book meeting rooms for themselves in order to have a quiet space to work in and finish their tasks. This is not a good use of space, according to managers, especially in offices where there is a constant need for space to make video calls and voice conferences with team members around the world. What I observed was a genuine need for more private, individual workspaces.

Food programs do not generate profit. The snacks, coffee, and meals all cost something, along with the cost of actually implementing the food programs. But these costs must be weighed against the social stigma of not providing free food in an industry where free food is, as I previously said, required.

No tech company wants to seem weird for not offering food. There was definitely competition for prestige and those that spent the most got the most, at least at the beginning. Google spent lavish amounts of money on food and benefits for employees, which forced others to follow suit in order to compete. Given Google's rise to popularity at the same time social media was becoming popular, news of its legendary perks spread even quicker. Keeping employees in the office, one might argue, has been part of success. To prove this point, in 2013, Yahoo ordered workers based at home back to the office in an attempt to turn around its poor financial performance. The CEO, Marissa Mayer, who was previously at Google, also gave employees free food and new smartphones. A lack of control was cited by the company as one of the reasons for the call back to the office (Miller 2013).

Mike, the manager at Company A in London, told me that it was important for people to be in the office—that it was an office-based company, solidifying Mayer's position of bringing employees back into the office. This essentially validates the idea that being in the office sustains the office itself and also, that having employees in the office creates a sense of control. Although there are companies that exist digitally, spread out around the globe linked only by cables and switches, I believe their ability to function as a company is limited. Bringing groups of people together in an office is key to creating and sustaining a company. Some, like Zuker, believe that without continuous action to maintain the existing order in these organizations, they risk "decaying into cultural artifacts" (Zucker 1988). Although I would not go that far, there is a delicate balance between flexibility and structure that these companies are trying to manage.

Mike is right, though. Employees need to be in the office to maintain the company. In the last days I spent before the Christmas break at Company A, the numbers started to dwindle as people took days off before the holiday.

By the final day, the office was a barren shell of what it usually was. Salespeople were not on the phone because their clients were also on holiday. The office was quiet, and, at times, I remarked in my notes that it felt more like a library—even the music was turned off. Food is part of creating a homey office culture when a major alternative is working from home.

To further understand the culture of free food in these offices, it's worth taking a look at a couple of food rituals that I observed as meaningful: snacks, coffee, and holiday meals.

On Snacks

Snacks are very, very important and individuals have very different opinions about what snacks the company offers. Google has even researched and "optimized office snacks" with published results (Chance et al. 2016). Studies have shown that snacks at work can make employees "happy" and that millennials actively seek out jobs that offer snacks (Malcolm 2015). Mintz discussed sugar, tea, coffee, rum, and tobacco as the great "proletarian hunger-killers" and in fact, some of the snacks within these offices definitely fit into that framework. Perhaps the best example of a modern-day tech office hunger killer is the granola bar or, to use the brand name, Cliff Bar. Filled with, yes, sugar, but also oats, nuts, dried fruit, and protein, its original use was for climbers, but it has transitioned into the mainstream diet and can be used as a meal replacement or boost (I ate them myself in some of the offices that provided them). Much like Mintz's suggestion that these substances became daily necessities by 1900, almost all tech employees I spoke to for this research feel the same about snacks (Mintz 2013, 94).

Most employees I spoke with about snacks thought that there was not a good balance between "unhealthy" snacks like potato chips and cookies, and healthy snacks like dried fruit, nuts, and granola bars—leaning too far to the healthy side. As a result, some employees even went so far as to bring in their own—usually "junk food." I observed one employee bringing in four liters of Coke Zero and placing it in the fridge for himself. This type of provisioning happens normally in other offices without snacks—employees might keep something in their desks or lockers for themselves. They have the ability to choose what to eat. The problem, then, is choice. Employees want more of a chance to influence what snacks they get. You might ask why these companies did not solicit opinions about what snacks to provide—they did not have to. Employees would freely and openly express their opinions to the food program managers whenever they could via email, gossip, or directly. There were audible gasps when Kim at Company A in London, after months of comments, finally bought pretzels for the snack bar.

Overall, each food program manager confessed that it is difficult to please everyone. "You can't do it," Charlotte said. "It is impossible; there will always be someone who is not happy." It is reminiscent, then, to running a prison. As a prison officer says in Bell and Valentine's book in reference to prisoners and food, "You won't please them all. But if you can keep the majority happy, it keeps the roof on your prison" (Bell and Valentine 1997). Charlotte, though, was not only tasked with snacks in San Francisco but had to respond to requests for more "tech snacks" from a newly acquired company's office in Amsterdam. "What are tech snacks?" I asked. "Snacks that showed guests that they were a tech company," she said. She mentioned products like vegan and organic granola bars, fresh fruit, nuts, and energy drinks.

This confirms that the snacks reflected not only employee preferences but also a style of consumption congruent with the company culture. Silicon Valley had exported not only technology to the world but a genre of snacks too. I should not have been surprised, given the number of journalistic articles about these companies' food perks and benefits. The new office was somehow validated through the snacks it offered, emulating Silicon Valley. Eating habits frame a national culture; taking away the snacks that those in Amsterdam might normally eat, in a way, cuts into their ability to remain Dutch. Nevertheless, it is consistent with the feeling of entitlement. Now that they were part of a US company, they felt entitled to specific types of snacks.

By giving food to employees from the get-go, companies have created a kind of moral economy, where employees expect food, and receiving it adds to the established custom between the company and its employees, and there is disgruntlement if this established norm is threatened. This is the opposite of a tribute (lower status to higher status), which, in turn, maintains the balance of power between the company and employee. The path Graeber suggests is that an action, repeated, becomes customary; it then defines the "actor's identity, their very nature" (Graeber 2014a, 74). This helps answer my own question about where a sense of entitlement comes from: it is now customary to receive free food. Breaking it means breaking an established set of actions and rules.

On LaCroix Water and Value

If there is one product that is in every tech office in San Francisco, it is La-Croix water. LaCroix is flavored sparkling water in a can. It is free from everything: sugar, sodium, calories, and preservatives. It comes in over twenty flavors. The favorite in tech circles is *Pamplemousse* (grapefruit). This is not a Mintz-sanctioned hunger killer: it has no calories and no sugar. First produced in Wisconsin in 1981, LaCroix has had an unusual path to stardom.

Trends in America normally filter in from the coasts—LaCroix did exactly the opposite. Why a French name for something made in America? Most sparkling water available in the United States was imported—Perrier and San Pellegrino being the two most popular—so it appears that the creators of LaCroix were eager to join the ranks of European sounding names. Also, Wisconsin has a history of using French words, especially in naming cities.[2]

When I landed in San Francisco, I found LaCroix everywhere—the offices, the supermarket, the convenience store, even the airport. Company A had several shelves in one of their fridges devoted to it; it needs almost constant restocking. Company B's office went through so much that it caused a recycling problem.

I could not write about food in the tech industry without mentioning La-Croix. It is just so prevalent in the industry that leaving it out would be akin to not mentioning coffee. Friends on Facebook report drinking it all the time at home. Articles have been written about it in the *New Yorker,* the *New York Times*, and *Vox Media* (Choi 2015, Nelson 2016, Marfield 2017). Numerous websites offer their own flavor ratings. LaCroix has its own merchandise. There are T-shirts, pins, and even watercolor paintings. How did this relatively mundane brand of sparkling water become a status symbol in the tech industry—part of employees' identities?

Graeber's theory of consumption and value, when applied to LaCroix water, is a way to understand how this "concrete medium" registers in the imagination of those who consume it (in this case, tech employees). We have to understand LaCroix's place in a larger system of what keeps these offices running (Graeber 2001, 31). The larger symbolic system consists of a number of alternative drinks like Coke, energy drinks, juice, coffee, tea, and plain tap water. Why choose LaCroix out of this lineup?

It is not necessarily cheap, but also not expensive. It is not that different from a number of other bottled carbonated waters (Perrier, San Pellegrino) except that it is not imported. It has no additives, sugar, or calories (it is "clean"). It is caffeine free. In economic terms, it would make more sense for employees to drink the most expensive products. However, those were often the last to be consumed. When LaCroix is running low or out of stock, employees notice and complain.

Nevertheless, I think a better way to consider this drink is as an object of transcendent value—one of the last things that these employees are willing to part with. These cans of drinks are not heirlooms. They are not valued because of their particular histories or the knowledge of the particular hands they have passed through. They are solidly alienated commodities. Nevertheless, LaCroix is a commodity that means an awful lot to these people (Weiner 1977, Mauss 1990). There are over 170,000 Instagram posts tagged with #lacroix or #lacroixwater.

LaCroix seems more to be connected to the party atmosphere of the tech workplaces and the focus on health, healthism, and the trend of "clean eating,"[3] since LaCroix really has nothing in it besides artificial flavoring, water, and CO_2.

But brands like Allbirds and LaCroix do more than serve as an object of transcendent value. They also signify people's tastes, and I would say that both Allbirds and LaCroix are forms of anti-fashion. This is what Daniel Miller would call "style—that is, the individual construction of an aesthetic based on not just what you wear, but how you wear it" (Miller 2013, 15). They work in different ways, the shoes signifying one's commitment to the sneaker-and-sweatshirt college dress code, an ethic of no-nonsense hard work, while also indexing wealth. It is a complex construction of the self—as Miller contends in his book. He argues that the sari actually constitutes who Indian women are, just as a pair of Allbirds shoes can constitute who a tech worker is.

I saw people drinking LaCroix at breakfast, lunch, and dinner as well as all times in between. They drank while standing, walking, sitting at their desks, chatting with colleagues at high round tables; they were even on the phones in some occasions. I never observed anyone open a can and pour it into a glass and no one used straws.

I saw people take two, or three at a time, presumably for colleagues or for their evening commute home. I watched people open the fridge, grab one, replace it, and grab a different flavor. I watched as the more popular flavors dwindled while the least popular ones remained (coconut). I tried coconut to see why it was always the last choice; it's because it tastes like drinking suntan lotion.

So, what is the value of this water? LaCroix is mostly about what it is not—not caffeinated, not sugary. Mary Choi confirms this in her article about LaCroix where she tells us, "LaCroix is everything-free: sugar, sodium, calorie, preservative" (Choi 2015). But what is missing from her analysis is the fact that LaCroix has a built-in community—people notice it if you're drinking it in a way that no one drinking Coke or Pepsi does. While drinking one in San Francisco at the Company B office, one of the employees told me to "try the lemon one." I had, and it was delicate and refreshing. Another employee at Company A warned me against the coconut flavor: "It tastes like the beach, and not in a good way." They were right. No one warns you about the sweetness of Cherry Coke or the strange artificial sugar taste in a Diet Pepsi. The community that LaCroix has built around its product (refer back to the number of Instagram posts) is a testament to its ability to be a cultural icon in an industry that has a strange affinity with cultural icons.

Allbirds is the other prime example. They are meaningful because they are not Nike, Adidas, or Reebok (or any other mass-produced product); they are meaningful for their complete lack of care about how you look in them. A 2019 article says that Allbirds are "footwear for people who poke around in the code on the websites they visit, and who would prefer not to think too hard about their footwear choices" (Caramanica 2019). It is as simple as the shoes are comfortable and durable, tick the boxes in most if not all of the ethical categories, and come in limited colors—and that they are $95. One wearer said they prefer the slip-on shoes because you can put them on faster—"they are more efficient" (Bowles 2018). In an industry where time is precious, every second counts.

Can we name anything in the financial industry, the education industry, the manufacturing industry, or the hospitality industry that has any of the same cultural iconography as this can of fizzy drink or these shoes?

Caffeinated Spaces

Coffee is a very important part of office culture (Horowitz 2011, Gay 2016, Doherty 2017, Chepik 2017). Free coffee is the lifeblood of the tech office. It is so common in office spaces that I hesitate to call it a perk, although the quality can vary greatly. It seems usual for Silicon Valley-based tech companies to scale up the coffee brand as the company grows and makes more money. At Facebook, as Martinez suggests, they moved past the generic "corporate roast" for Philz Coffee—what he calls the "locavore's coffeehouse." By the time Martinez left Facebook, they had their own Philz location on the company's campus (Martinez 2016, 265).

Caffeine has been the stimulant of sociability for centuries—technology might change that, but it is still true in many offices around the western world (Anderson 2014). Having coffee around is a convenience for employees: it fights boredom and fatigue. Some even say that the appearance of a coffee cup near your workspace gives the appearance of productivity and busyness—it signals to others that you need a boost, that you've been working hard. I wanted to appear available for anyone to approach when I was in the office, but I also wanted to build rapport and fit in, so having coffee on my desk or in my hand was a double-edged sword.

D'Costa tells us that:

> We consume coffee as a means of performing the tasks we need to complete in the setting of the workplace. And if we all do it, then it normalizes the behavior and helps us believe that we are achieving optimal levels of productivity. (D'Costa 2011)

Coffee is held in high esteem in the Bay Area. Home to a number of specialty roasters, coffee is a serious business. Like sports teams, coffee brands have die-hard fans—they wear T-shirts and hats with the company logo and have loyalty cards.[4, 5]

But as Roseberry points out, the connections that consumers and individuals have toward different coffee brands or styles have actually been carefully constructed by the market:

> That is to say, my newfound freedom to choose and the taste and discrimination I cultivate, have been shaped by traders and marketers responding to a long-term decline in sales with a move toward market segmentation along class and generational lines. . . . This is not, of course, to say we enter the market as mere automatons; clearly, we have and exercise choices, and we (apparently) have more things to choose from than we once did. But we exercise those choices in a world of structured relationships, and part of what those relationships structure (or shape) is both the arena and the process of choice itself. (Roseberry 1996, 771)

The concerned interest shown by workers in tech offices about their coffee warrants the detailed attention I give it here, so it is important to know what each office had available in terms of coffee. I am a coffee drinker and, in my opinion, the office with the best coffee was the Company B office in San Francisco (more on that in just a moment).

Coffee Arrangements in Each Office

- Company A, London.
  - Free, unlimited coffee and tea. The coffee came from an automated espresso machine that would even make cappuccinos. Real china cups, no paper cups available.
  - Coffee brand—unknown.
- Company A, San Francisco
  - Free, unlimited, filter-style coffee was brewed constantly when the office was open. Each corner of the office had a small coffee station with two to three different brews, condiments, and reusable cups.
  - In the central part of the office, next to the smoothie room, there was an espresso machine manned by a full-time barista who would make any coffee you wanted.
  - Coffee brand—Philz.
- Company B, London
  - Free, unlimited coffee was provided from automated espresso machines. Real china cups, no disposable cups. One located in the kitchen and one located upstairs at the small snack bar.
  - Coffee brand—unknown.

Figure 4.1. L to R: Coffee machine Company A, London, Coffee machine Company B, London, Coffee machine Company B, Dublin

- Company B, Dublin
  - Free, unlimited coffee was provided from automated espresso machines. One in each of the two kitchens, and one in a small snack bar area. Real china and ceramic cups, no disposable cups.
  - Coffee brand—Blue Tiger Coffee.
- Company B, San Francisco
  - Free, unlimited coffee was provided.
  - Brew methods varied. There was a Chemex pour-over pot, a traditional filter coffeepot, several French-press pots, a manual espresso machine, and an AeroPress. Employees took turns making coffee when they desired. Real cups either brought from home or provided by Company B. No disposable cups.
  - Coffee brand—Blue Bottle (although this was in the process of changing).

The Coffee Argument

It was a quiet afternoon in San Francisco the day the news dropped that Company B was cutting free lunch to once a week and reviewing all food-related costs. The news travelled fast through the office—Hannah, the office food manager, had sent out an email to all employees communicating the changes and shared the news with me verbally.

I was sitting on the sofa near the kitchen that day, writing some notes and overheard a conversation between Hannah and several of the employees about the announcement. It was company-wide, she mentioned. Every office would be making "sacrifices." The main topic of conversation that afternoon was what coffee brand they would switch to—currently, they served Blue Bottle, one of the most expensive brands of coffee available and nearly everyone was happy with it. However, Hannah needed to reduce costs and there were a number of other boutique roasters that cost less.

But it was not that simple.

As I sat there observing, opinions about which coffee to buy were thrown around the room like rockets. Mild arguments broke out as the conversation dragged more and more people into it. Voices rose from the kitchen as each person was trying to one-up the other. I sat there amazed at the amount of time, energy, and emotion these employees were able to put into this. It gave me my first glimpse of the seriousness with which people take their coffee, brand loyalty, and also once again the idea of entitlement. Nevertheless, as Hannah confessed to me later on, there was "no way I could ever get rid of coffee all together." This was surprising, since Company B was trying to engage with the surrounding community and just outside there were more places to get coffee than I could count, not to mention that small cafes are struggling in the center of San Francisco—a result of how much tech employees were getting for free at work. To me, this was an opportunity to put Company B's priorities, mission, and philosophy to a test. Coffee, though, is seen as such an essential part of office culture that not having it would put Company B into the category of weird and strange, not to mention that it would be very hard to recruit anyone to work there.

The conversation went something like this, with Hannah telling me about the coffee situation and others in the kitchen jumping in to comment:

Hannah: With the new budget, I'm going to have to re-think the coffee we're buying. Blue Bottle is the most expensive and there are a lot of good alternatives out there.

Employee 1: Just don't get Philz. It's the worst. My friend at [another tech company] has it and they just tell me how bad it is.

Employee 2: Philz is good, but I wouldn't say the best. I mean, it's obviously not as good as Blue Bottle, so if we have to get something cheaper, then Philz is an obvious choice.

Hannah: I'm going to look into a lot of options and see what kinds of prices we can get. We go through so much coffee here.

Employee 1: The beans have to be good, though. If they are dry or old—well, you know some of us use the pour-over in the morning so . . . Blue Bottle is too corporate now anyway.

Hannah: I'll do my best to get samples in and then maybe we can have a taste test session.

Employee 1: I'm telling you; everyone has Philz now, and it's no good. It's not like getting it at the cafe. It's not like Philz is "local" anymore. I mean, they opened up in Los Angeles and DC now.

Employee 2: Does it have to be a local roaster? There are some great coffee roasters in Portland—like . . .

Hannah: I was thinking of trying Ritual Roasters, or maybe Sightglass?

Employee 2: Sightglass is great, but I doubt it's less than Blue Bottle.

Employee 1: Four Barrel, then. That's my vote.

Hannah: I can't please everyone—maybe I'm just going to have to get Starbucks and we can use the leftover money for better or more snacks.

Employee 1: You *can't* get Starbucks—really, I mean, are they cutting the budget that much? We can't serve people Starbucks here—like a hotel? I mean, really—it's as bad a Folgers. There has to be some give . . .

Employee 2: I totally agree!

This coffee argument illustrates the idea of consumption habits that drive identity via products. From Graeber we can understand that "real working people find most of their life's treasures in consumption . . . [and] they create their own meaning out of the products with which they choose to surround themselves" (Graeber 2011, 490). What I witnessed was a response to what was perceived as an attack on a product that gives special meaning to these employees in that Company B office—a specific brand of coffee. West, in her book about coffee production in Papua New Guinea, discusses what she calls "neoliberal coffee," detailing the ways in which different generations of consumers perceive coffee brands, brewing, and the industry in general. Based on her analysis, Martin would fall somewhere between baby boomers and generation X, meaning that he had values like optimism, teamwork, and personal growth, while also adhering to ideas of what West calls "liquid value," those who can adjust to anything and have no respect for authority (West 2012, 35).

In her book, West is actually quoting from a conference of the Specialty Coffee Association of America's meeting, where a man she calls "Mr. Nebraska" is describing consumer production to the crowd (descriptions that West rejects). But I find his descriptions of values for each group of people really enlightening and helpful when considering how coffee is perceived and how it is valued. According to him (coming from West's book), millennials are defined by a certain list of events like the Oklahoma City bombing, 9/11, and the Columbine shootings. He adds that they want "achievement but are not driven, value globalism but are community focused and think that by looking inward they can change the world" as well as being encoded with a desire for brands and logos and look for global products that are "political and environmentally friendly" (West 2012, 35).

English-Lueck, talking about corporate care in Silicon Valley, touches on this phenomenon, even without explicitly stating it.

> Both food and work are markers of class identity and morality, so it is no surprise that corporate food would concern such distinctions. Culinary individualism, flexible work and eating schedules, cosmopolitan cuisine and a progressive morality of foodscapes combine to create a new regime of distinction. Counter to industrial food design based on modularity and mass commodification, new food niches reflect more customized tastes, needs and desires. (English-Lueck et al. 2014, 39)

Coffee brands are a definitive marker of class distinction in contemporary consumer culture (Bookman 2013, 406). Opinions expressed by everyone in the office about what coffee they should have were small ways of proving their own cultural capital. Coffee is polarizing—there was no way that Hannah could have said, "I'm going to buy Folgers." She also had to live with her choice and had her own strong opinions about coffee. Taste in coffee can work to reinforce class boundaries, but that is not what was happening here. This was entitlement in its purest form—entitled to coffee—entitled to good coffee—entitled to the best coffee—as chosen by me. No one had a taste for "ordinary" or "standard" coffee, that is, supermarket brands like Folgers. Even Starbucks was a non-starter due to its gross commercialization. The conversation eventually calmed down with no real resolution. I knew Hannah had her hands full trying to please everyone while also balancing the even slimmer budget she had to work with.

The conversation about coffee in Company B's London office showed a different, very mundane side. No one cared what the brand was, and, in fact, I never found out. The truth is, the brand did not matter at all; it just mattered that there *was* coffee. Even if London as a city has a similar counter-culture-coffee industry, you do not feel that in the office as you do in San Francisco. What I found in London was that employees would regularly go out for a coffee. It gave them a break, a reason to go outside, and acted as a bonding exercise. I went with employees on many of these trips and drank countless cups of coffee as a result.

It seemed that coffee choice in the office in London carried fewer stigmas than those in San Francisco. Not only did the choice of what coffee to serve in the San Francisco office represent to the employees the health of the company financially, but to an outsider visiting (say from a vendor or another tech company) offering them a low-quality cup of coffee would signal something dire—because everyone in the tech world is obviously attuned to the coffee scene. It is all about the image projected to the outside world, especially in San Francisco. Coffee is a status symbol.

Maybe this is part of the civilizing process of the San Francisco tech community—part of the shifting in the thresholds of repugnance. Elias was not wrong in citing his understanding of how small changes in etiquette and manners in the upper classes filtered down to the lower classes (the fork!) (Elias 1978, 68). Coffee is no different in this regard. Even Starbucks is following more high-end, third-wave coffee trends (pour-over, Chemex, etc.).

One day, I noticed that an employee had his own bag of coffee beans on his desk. I did not hesitate to ask him about it. He told me he didn't like the long, drip filter style of coffee that was brewed constantly in the office. Instead, he brought his own coffee from home and brewed it himself in the way he preferred, in an AeroPress. Actions speak loud here; I had only been in the office for a few days, and I noticed that he was the only one showcasing his coffee on his desk—this is a reality of not having any drawers or personal storage space—but also because he was identifying himself with an elevated way of brewing coffee and not with, what he considered, inferior coffee brewed for the rest of the employees. He is defining his membership in a different, possibly more superior group, via coffee (Anderson 2014). Meanwhile, back in the Company B office, Hannah was considering Philz coffee as a solid replacement for Blue Bottle, which proved to be a polarizing choice.

Office managers have a peculiar role in the overall organization of the office. Hannah was the liaison between any food and drink vendor and the company. She was responsible for the design of the kitchen, keeping it stocked, and choosing suppliers aligned with Company B's core principals—a difficult task. When asked, the office and food managers are responsible, essentially, for maintaining employee happiness within a budget. These women (Kim, Hannah, Jennifer, Katie) must keep employees fed. Each one recounted to me in interviews the challenge of keeping people happy as well as the stretching of a budget. But more than just managing budgets, much of their work goes unseen much like the planning and management of a family meal in a domestic setting where there is a sense that doing the work well means maintaining some kind of invisibility that people are often unable to, or reluctant to talk about (DeVault 2013, 182).

The actual work of buying and sourcing the food, snacks, and drinks are tasks that are not observed or understandable by most others in the office. To be fair, lots of jobs in these offices are unseen, because most are done digitally. But it does show that there is a kind of preconceived way that providing food is considered. What I don't want to imply here is that these roles were filled by women because of a gender role-based hiring strategy. They are jobs that anyone with the right skills could do. The more interesting point is that they just happened to be all women, and that they were also the "go-to" person for other issues, which does relate back to the idea of the mother/wife who has been identified as the household manager in so many past studies.[6]

These women were also involved in the coding and decoding of the messages sent by the foods that were available in the offices. What do I mean? They controlled the meaning behind giving employees burgers or a salad. Each of those transmits something different. At Company B in London, this was particularly true in the types of foods that Jennifer chose. It was nearly all vegetarian (message: meat is bad) and tended to be very low on carbs (message: lighter is better). Nearly all the snacks were organic (message: organic is better/healthier). These were not necessarily truths, but the position that the company wanted to represent—Jennifer was the translator.

The idea of food as code was explored in depth by Mary Douglas, who argued that if "food is treated as a code, the message it encodes will be found in the pattern of social relations being expressed" (Douglas 1972, 61). Her argument tells us that through the coding of food, the messages that are sent have primarily to do with inclusion/exclusion, boundaries, and levels of hierarchy. The position the company is representing has more to do with the physical health of the employees than, as a comparison, the spiritual health. Where Douglas talks about the Jewish custom of avoiding pigs, here we have the Company B custom of avoiding non-organic foods. Yet, there is no social, moral, or spiritual repercussions for eating non-organic foods. The decoded meal, in this case, does not represent a "stern, tragic religion" (Douglas 1972, 79).

What Anderson says about this issue is that cultural foodways have to be predictable and comprehensible if they are to have any communicative value (Anderson 2014). Food can convey subtle and complex messages. This is what these women were facilitating. In contrast to language, messages about food tend to be less precise, instead of conveying broad and deep ideas. Though there is one message that food makes clear and that is its connection with home, family, and security. But when we review the photographs of these spaces, look at the food, view the ways in which the food is presented and displayed, how snacks are stacked: does it give you a warm feeling of home and comfort? These spaces are sterile, stark offices that give off a generic feeling of corporate design and efficiency. They are very un-home-like and only comfortable in the sense that they provide shelter from the elements, a place to eat away from the masses, and a feeling of comfort that comes from having a space to work at to call your own. Now, we hear of companies like Facebook and Google building large, developed communities in Silicon Valley where employees will not only be able to work for these companies but live in housing that the companies own and manage. It is one more step in the direction to blur work and non-work spaces. It shows just how complex life is becoming for these employees; it is a return to the company towns of the twentieth century, like Hershey, Pennsylvania; Corning, New York; or Gary, Indiana (Streitfeld 2018).

Holidays, Ritual, and Thanksgiving Abroad

Holiday food rituals are important cultural artifacts. For Americans, Thanksgiving is a holiday that is bursting at the seams with rituals. It is a highly symbolic consumption event with specific scripts and roles. There is less latitude for interpretation regarding what is appropriate than an ordinary meal (Marshall 2005, 76).

I happened to be in London for Thanksgiving and celebrated Thanksgiving lunch in the Company A office there (the head office in the United States was closed). We celebrated in the office with a larger than normal, catered meal. From my field notes, I have chronicled this very American ritual as one of the only Americans present.

The delivery driver is about to leave: "I'll be back tomorrow to collect the pans," he says as he heads out the door. Kim places the metal trays full of food along the kitchen table and slowly peels off the foil from the turkey. The smell hits me, just a few feet away at my desk. Next, she opens up the green beans, the roasted potatoes, and the pumpkin. "I got a few different pies at Waitrose," she says, gesturing to a row of desserts waiting under red paper napkins on the windowsill. I get up to see the food and help out preparing.

The office has been decorated in red and white, with Christmas crackers set all along the table at each place setting. In America, we use orange, brown, tan, yellow, and black at Thanksgiving. Christmas crackers don't exist. There is Christmas music playing on the speakers, the TV at the end of the long table is showing a film and then changes to a screen saver of a fireplace. It feels wrong—something is off—but the food smells right.

It's about twelve noon on Thursday, the 24th of November, and we are about to celebrate American Thanksgiving in the office of Company A in London. The American headquarters in San Francisco are closed today, so the London office is celebrating the American holiday. I am one of three Americans here for the meal—and so I field a lot of questions. "Are these the right decorations?" (Not really) "What kind of music should we play? Christmas?" (No!) "What's Thanksgiving about?" (Long story . . .) Etc.

In the kitchen, a few guys are standing around making punch. "Try this, it's from Poland," giving me a shot of vodka. "We're mixing it with pear juice and cider with some sliced apples and pears inside." The boozy combination will probably put us all to sleep after the meal, but it's definitely a nice gesture on this cold day.

The food is all displayed, steam rising from the trays. Kim calls for everyone, it's just past 12, the normal lunchtime. It is one of the few days of the year when they all eat together—normally, the food arrives, and people eat as they can, a majority at 12, but a few later on. A line forms for the food, people pile their plates full of turkey, stuffing, beans, potatoes, and pumpkin, grab a glass of punch, and sit down at a long table that has been pieced together out of many different parts of the office. We're all there together, there is jazz playing on the speakers, and the smells of Thanksgivings past come to mind—sitting at my grandmother's table with my cousins, the smell of turkey and butter, the whiff of cinnamon and apples. A pot of coffee brewing.

Before dessert, as we were all sitting in our food-funded daze, we went around the table to say what we were thankful for—a nice tradition that many families in the US practice (although usually *before* you start eating). "This nice meal," says one, "our new office," says another. And so, it goes on until the pies get cut and we all dig into dessert.

Thanksgiving is a holiday that is grounded in food—it is the food that allows for the cultural survival of the holiday.

I witnessed this firsthand in London where, without the assistance of Americans, with just basic knowledge that the food has to be specific, they successfully pulled off an American Thanksgiving meal. If the food were wrong, it would have thrown off the entire event. The cultural significance of Thanksgiving food has been well documented, at least in America, but abroad there are countless places where Americans who live in different cities or countries are looking for ingredients to make "Mom's pumpkin pie" or "turkey and noodles." Cranberries are notoriously hard to find. Kohn covered this well in her article chronicling her own Thanksgiving experiences abroad as a way of understanding "a couple of key components of the American Thanksgiving meal and how they travel, and on how diversity of experience is embodied in the methods and ingredients for producing the bird and the pie" (Kohn 2013, 52). Here, the grocery store chain Whole Foods Market caters to the large American community in London by providing a source for many of the brands and ingredients you find elsewhere in America. Even Tesco carries marshmallows (an important ingredient for yams and marshmallows) and Libby's pumpkin pie in a can (the only brand that any decent American would use). I'm not the only one to notice the significance of pumpkin pie to Americans abroad—Kohn also notes that the pie is a "widely understood signifier for the Thanksgiving feast" (Kohn 2013, 54).

Apart from the ritual of the meal, the maintenance of the holiday, and the strangeness of celebrating it in the office of an American company in London, it was essentially about feeding employees. Thursday is a day when employees get food, usually a "cheat" day, where perhaps burgers, fried chicken, or meat of some kind is served. The employees, without recognizing the significance of the holiday, seemed to treat it as any other day of the week. After helping to clean up the mess and tidy things, everyone went back to work, back to their desks, back to their phone calls and meetings. This is against the grain of what normally happens at home on Thanksgiving. It felt so wrong to me to be back at the desk writing these field notes when all I could think about was how we should all be having a nap before starting to graze around the food again while a football game plays on the TV.

Near the end of the day, I helped pack up some of the food; there were a lot of leftovers. I told Kim that leftovers are the best part, and that people should be encouraged to take them home. There's enough for everyone to get something to take back. She nodded her head in semi-agreement.

Finally, at the end of the afternoon, the cleaning lady came, and was offered some food—she just laughed and said she'd take some with her. At the end of the day, I left but didn't take any food with me.

Thanksgiving, as a holiday, carries messages of identity, bonds with home, and memories of family. Eating a Thanksgiving meal in an office in London is a very strange way to celebrate it. I would argue that its place in American society and culture is more important than that of any other holiday.

I asked if the company celebrated English holidays in America. The answer was no. There is no Burns Night or Pancake Day celebration—no Queen's Birthday or May Bank Holiday to speak of. These celebrations do have some food traditions associated with them but that is not the point. By giving English employees a Thanksgiving meal, they are naturally extending the values and rituals of American culture into that office.

This works in favor of the company by creating an environment where employees can start to understand each other—what Brown and Mussell call communities of affiliation (Brown and Mussell 1984).

Most exported American culture comes from Hollywood—media, movies, TV, music, and popular culture. But it can also come via food. Look at the growth outside of the United States of companies like McDonald's, KFC, Burger King, and Subway. Company A is doing the same with their own food program, which promotes a certain kind of American tech office way of eating—let's call it gastro-tech-ology. This kind of lay gastronomy of Silicon Valley is creeping into the offices of tech companies around the world. Most of it is based on the cuisine of Northern California, where many tech companies begin. What is disturbing is that it has the possibility to change the ways in which people in other countries eat at work and it faces off against their own foodways.

Individuals construct their own personal foodways in the office, like the employee who brought his own coffee to work or the one who brought Coke Zero. Adapting to what is available, individual intention determines actual food consumption. (Anderson 2014)

That said, it is true that the office managers and owners can persuade or force people to eat particular things in particular ways (Anderson 2014). The gastronomy of Silicon Valley and Northern California somehow has become the de facto gastronomy of the tech industry. They are influencing eating habits, and this is a clear display of power and agency.

> Foucault could have found as much evidence for this in foodways as he did in his studies of the history of sexuality. However, people can learn and resist. The result is a negotiation, not a stable and fixed "construction." (Anderson 2014)

There must be ways in which local cuisines (and mealtimes) are adapted into the tech office. Although my research did not take me into offices in countries with well-established food cultures, like Japan, Italy, or Spain, one can imagine that in these countries you would find a different set of foods, different eating times, and different personally constructed foodways.

What I argue, then, is that countries with a lesser established national culture of gastronomy are more susceptible to fluctuating ways of eating and thus open to the gastronomy of the tech office. Some might claim that these, mostly Anglo-Saxon countries do have a food culture, but what they most often refer to is the result of immigration which has helped to form part of their national cuisine.

In London, I got the opportunity to visit a company that offers its employees a free vegetarian lunch cooked in the office by a couple of chefs. The company, while tech-focused, actually produces the physical objects they design. The office was crowded, but each day at lunchtime they would all sit around long tables that had been set for lunch. Before eating, they clapped in appreciation for the chefs (who were merely doing their job). After lunch, I talked with a few employees who told me that lunch reminded them of being in primary school and that none of them really understood the clapping—most found it patronizing. "Did you hear about the washing-up roster?" one of them asked. "No, what's that?" I replied. There was a schedule for washing up that each employee was on. This type of labor is not normally part of someone's workday in an office.

This particular office is a good example of a food program that was not attempting to please the employees. It was a food program based on the food philosophy of the founder. There was some talk of food programs like this in San Francisco—in fact, I unsuccessfully tried to gain access to one. It resembled a prison or hospital where inmates have no consent in what they eat. But here is where there is room for subversion—the group that dodged the lunch meal to go out for something with meat or the employee who did not adhere to the washing-up schedule, which I was told happened all too often.

It is evident from the discussion above that food inside these spaces has some control over the employees, but in each location that control acts out differently. In the next chapter, I will discuss the importance of space and its relationship to commensality in these offices.

NOTES

1. This is reminiscent of Adam Smith's book, *The Theory of Moral Sentiments*, where he labels this the "impartial spectator."

2. See Eau Claire, Allouez, Belmont, Beloit, Des Plaines River, Pepin, St. Croix Falls, Lac Vieux Desert, etc.

3. Clean eating is a complicated, ever-changing idea that you should be eating "clean" food, though there is no official definition as to what that means. Now, though, for every article telling you that sparkling water is okay, there is one that is warning you about the hidden dangers in your next can of LaCroix. See https://www.shape.com/healthy-eating/healthy-drinks/why-your-lacroix-obsession-isnt-healthy.

4. These shirts and caps are available to purchase at https://www.philzcoffee.com/shop/merchandise. https://bluebottlecoffee.com/store/gifts.

5. Coffee in San Francisco can be very expensive. It is a real financial commitment to frequent any of the specialty coffee shops in the Bay Area. The average price of a small cappuccino in San Francisco is $3.60 USD (https://www.baristamagazine.com/average-cost-coffee/).

6. For more on this see Berk's *The Gender Factory: The Appointment of Work in American Households* (1985), Charles and Kerr's *Women, Food and Families* (1960), Hartman's *The Family as the Locus of Gender, Class, and Political Struggle: The Example of Housework* (1981), and Hochschild's *The Second Shift: Working Parents and the Revolution at Home* (1989).

Chapter Five

Why Space Matters

Walking down Strand Street in central Dublin, I noticed the dodgy looking bar at the end of the road and the way in which the brick buildings resembled docklands. There were no benches, and the sidewalks were narrow, meaning if I met someone going the opposite direction, one of us would have to step into the street. But luckily, the passage was quiet, despite being just steps away from some of the most touristy parts of town. A discreet logo on the outside of the building signaled the name of the company housed inside: Company B. The grey/black bricks encased the office space where large windows on the second and third floors look out onto the street below and at the office buildings across the way. From the outside, it seemed quaint and welcoming—much more so than a glass and steel monolith or a boxy one-floor warehouse space does.

On entering the building, I was greeted with plants and pendant lights hung from the ceiling. Small knickknacks were on trendy-looking tables, instantly telling me where I was—this is Company B, it's cute and crafty. The old wooden stairs creaked under my weight as I climbed to the next floor up, where the receptionist who doubles as the security guard waits. She/he gave me the introduction to the office, a badge, and the non-disclosure agreement to sign before I entered, the same one I've signed before in the other offices. The iPad remembered my name and email address and then told me the Wi-Fi password; again, it was the same as in every other office. The interior was divided into several floors and old oak beams on the ceiling gave it a very modern, yet comfortable feeling. There was a lot of natural light. Employees sat at long wooden desks, divided only by their computers and personal effects—essentially a lot like the long wooden tables on the top floor where they gather together to eat lunch each day at 1 p.m. The floor was made up of wood planks, reminiscent of a ship. I later learned that the building was a former warehouse and was listed as a historic building.

This space was excellent for creating a sense of belonging and purpose through the use of materials that made you feel like the company behind the renovations actually cared about the employees working there. The complete lack of cubicles, plastic chairs, or tables, the attention to details like natural light, plants, and wood meant that employees were embedded into an environment that they might actually like to stay in—the bottom line is that it was very homey but also conformed to Company B's philosophy of using natural and organic products. The idea of home seems to be what many of these companies are trying to achieve with their dining spaces, not just via the physical environments they create, but also through the food they serve.

Figure 5.1.   L: Company B's dining area in Dublin. R: My lunch.

What do we look for in an office? What are the key characteristics that generate feelings of comfortableness, difference, and energy to work, but encourage us to leave at the end of the day? The philosopher Alain de Botton says that home can be "an airport or a library, a garden or a motorway diner" (De Botton 2008, 107)—why not an office, then?

TRAPPED IN AN OPEN OFFICE

Working in these companies nearly always means you have a lack of personal space. The degradation of the personal office or cubicle in these workplaces has created a sense of observation—the exact opposite of freedom. Freedom implies that you can do what you want when you want, and to some extent this is the case. Many employees set their own schedules and work from home on occasion. But the feeling of being observed has only increased through the use of technology, the very industry these employees work in. The impression of having more "agency" or freedom is key to the industry, which seems to pride itself on re-inventing what it means to be an office worker (Konnikova 2014, Surowiecki 2014, 425).

But that freedom that some feel comes through things like an open office, which might help to create a symbolic sense of organizational mission, making employees feel like part of a more laid-back, innovative enterprise, but can actually be damaging to the "workers' attention spans, productivity, creative thinking, and satisfaction" (Konnikova 2014). Psychologically, the repercussions of open offices are relatively straightforward. Physical barriers have been closely linked to psychological privacy, and a sense of privacy boosts job performance. Open offices also remove an element of control, which can lead to feelings of helplessness (Konnikova 2014).

Even so, nearly 70 percent of office spaces now have an open floor plan. The open office produces a tangible sense of surveillance. As an anthropologist, I wanted to be open and available, yet I increasingly felt pressured to

Figure 5.2. Brunch at Company A, San Francisco

look busy because I felt observed. Even if I wasn't an employee, the way the office was arranged gave me the same feeling of a lack of privacy Konnikova talks about. That's not to mention the constant interruptions or problems of concentration due to the number of people on the phone or the constant stream of music playing from the speakers.[1]

It was a morning like many others in San Francisco—foggy and cool, but with the sun trying to burn through. I rode the elevator up to the Company A office. The doors opened and I turned right to walk out into the main reception area. I greeted the receptionist there and smelled, on this day, something familiar and promising, cooked bacon, maple syrup, the slight aroma of coffee. "Are you joining us for brunch today?" she asked, like she was ready to walk me to my table. "I suppose I am," I answered.

I muddled around the office nursing a cup of coffee paying close attention to the food service workers preparing the morning's meal. The smell was overwhelming now and hard to ignore. Brunch was served from 11 a.m. until 2 p.m. and, at a few minutes to eleven, I lined up with the rest of the employees. I proceeded to load my plate with pancakes, bacon, sausages, and a heavy dose of maple syrup. From there I filled my coffee mug with some Philz's black java and took a seat. The conversations ranged from the food to weekend plans. I noticed one girl talking about how she disliked brunch because it's the day that "everyone brings everyone to show off." It seemed crazy the first time I heard about it, but it's common practice in most tech companies with free food: guests are welcome—even encouraged—to be part of a meal. Who takes part in these meals, this commensal activity, though, is highly significant. Brunch day at Company A, San Francisco, was the most popular day for guests to come to eat. Brunch is a very friendly meal if a meal can be called friendly—you know that almost anyone is going to like it. Most of all, it feels like a meal you might have at home and maybe that was the point, to make the employees realize that they can be at home in the office. It should feel as comfortable as their own home; why else would employees want to bring their parents and friends to work to eat?

Inviting guests to eat with you has been discussed by countless anthropologists, but the most striking and still-used examples are from Levi-Strauss and Mary Douglas, where they showed that the insider/outside concept for understanding how commensality functions is a way to understand boundaries within groups. By understanding symbolic boundaries, we can come to recognize "the lines that include and define some people, groups, and things while excluding others" (Epstein 1992, 232) and the link between, what Douglas calls the "system of social control expressed through the body and through observable artifacts of everyday life (food, dirt and material possessions)"

(Lamont et al. 2015, 851). Unlike a lot of the work in anthropology though, the everyday commensality that is at play in the offices of Company A and Company B is usually overlooked for those relating to religion, ritual, and sacrificial commensal events. Parents, friends, other family members share little to no commonality with those they eat with apart from their own familial bonds—yet, they are still sitting at the table and sharing a meal, which only enhances the significance of it (Simmel et al. 1997).

Sharing food is a clear sign of closeness while refusing to share is a clear sign of distance. These companies are trying to shorten the distance between themselves, their employees, and the public, yet the presence of a security guard or receptionist who allows access tells a different story. At Company A in San Francisco, located in a large multi-floor office building with multiple companies inside, the security guard was on the ground floor near the elevators. Each day I had to go through the process of getting permission to go upstairs, and it was only on the second or third week that the guard actually knew me and just waved me through. The problem was the elevator—I needed his keycard to allow me access to the Company A floor.

Inviting guests to share a meal is one way companies are attempting to mitigate a sense of distance—albeit only after guests take a photo of themselves and also sign a hefty non-disclosure agreement for fear that they are not just guests, but also spies, reporters, or employees from another company (or maybe a researcher). Bloch talks about the idea of commensality and poisoning, that choosing to eat with strangers who treat you like family means that you are relying on them not to poison you—you trust them, they trust you—but there is always a risk (Bloch 1999, 147). No tech company would dare poison someone that comes into the office to eat, but there are a number of similarities between the two that we can draw out here, namely that the idea of trust in one person or a group to not poison you is connected in these offices to the food program manager, who is the one who chooses the foods, meals, and drinks and is seen as the one who provides them, even if they are not in the kitchen cooking. That position exercises great power in these offices because they alone are the link between what the leaders have in mind for their employees and how those ideas and budgets get translated into reality—into food, into meals, into waste. They are the promoters of conviviality.

Yet, there is a difference between conviviality and commensality. Conviviality seems to be inherently related to positivity in most academic and non-academic studies. In order to understand commensality, we have to think about the ways in which society organizes itself by division—in the tech office, the "society" is divided by department, gender, work groups, hierarchy, and geographical spaces. Grignon says that "commensality is really social morphology" and so we must take into account "group relationships [that] take the practical shape of drink and food exchange, and of everything that is exchanged through this exchange" (Scholliers 2001, 25). Commensality is a more formal expression of hierarchy and dependence, which Mary Douglas discussed in her treatise on food events in her own home, telling us, "Drinks are for strangers, acquaintances, workmen and family. Meals are for family, close friends and honored guests" (Douglas 1972, 66).

Applying these ideas to the modern-day tech office, though, means that we have to "buck the trend" of happy thinking about how much conviviality and commensality mean to the workers, the corporate philosophy, and the public façade of these companies. The constant barrage of positive remarks about free meals at work does little to highlight the important circumstance of division and hides the institutional aspects of dining at work. "Institutions form us, and one can't help but judge the result," says Matthew B. Crawford (Crawford 2015). Without those inputs, we are left with a one-sided view of the dining practices inside these corporations. The article "Team Building in the Cafeteria" is the perfect example of the milieu of articles that highlight the positive side of eating together—of forced commensality. The article, which comes from the *Harvard Business Review*, tells us that many companies want to work to create "higher-performing, more cohesive teams" and that there is an incredibly simple way to do that: encourage teams to eat together (Kniffin et al. 2015). It draws on a study of firefighters, asking the question: "Do firefighters who eat together do their jobs better than those who don't?" They find that it does, but also note that the firefighters are not just eating together but also cooking together. There is an entire domestic arrangement that has been created within a fire department that an office just can't support—who is going to live at the office? In passing, there are a few negative sides, which are downplayed in the article, namely insularity, a pressure to conform, and managing out low performers. This is the division, the area of commensality that is passed over for the broader positive effects of eating together.

Fedele Bauccio, the founder of Bon Appetit Management company, with Google as one of its main clients, tells us that making great food and great food experiences can make employees "happier and more productive" (Bauccio 2013). Again, writing in the *Harvard Business Review*, the keywords focus on productivity, happiness, and inclusion. Happiness is a terribly hard thing to measure let alone understand from an empirical perspective. Bauccio, though, understands that food is not enough, space matters increasingly as well, and so we are told about Google's headquarters where you can eat fish tacos from a food truck parked outside or sit down at a what appears to be a traditional Indian restaurant located inside the office. Reservations can be made, waiters serve the food, you can even host a birthday party there—all for free as part of their food program.

But these pliant media outlets like the *Harvard Business Review*, the *New York Times*, *Slate*, *The Atlantic*, *Monocle*, and so on, are all part of a media circus that flatters the existing system by telling readers that it's the future. It's not—at least, not for future offices in Silicon Valley.

Two articles from 2018, one in the *New York Times* and one in the *San Francisco Chronicle*, address future free food programs in new tech offices in Silicon Valley and San Francisco. They report that understanding that there is a downside for the communities when employees don't leave the office, local governments are starting to take aim at perks, like free food, and clamp down on them for fear that the companies will only continue to serve themselves, more than the community itself. One article stated:

> Two San Francisco supervisors introduced an ordinance that would forbid employee cafeterias in new corporate construction. It is not clear whether the measure will pass, but it is a direct attack on one of the modern tech industry's most entrenched traditions. The ordinance, which seeks to force tech workers out of their subsidized cafeterias and into neighborhood restaurants, is the latest attempt by San Francisco leaders to make the tech companies that are migrating north from Silicon Valley adapt to life in the city. (Bowles 2018)

The other covers a similar issue:

> New companies such as Facebook and LinkedIn matched the perk as they tried to lure employees away. Staffing the cafeterias became a booming business for the formerly sleepy field of corporate catering. But the in-house eating places have drawn customers and potential employees away from neighboring businesses, and city officials are concerned that local restaurants struggle, and potentially bustling streets are empty as a result.
>
> Under Mountain View's rules for the Village complex, meals within the offices can't be subsidized by more than 50 percent on a regular basis. Facebook can fully subsidize employees if they go to restaurants that are open to the public. "It really was geared more around trying to make sure we didn't have 400,000 square feet of office space with people that never left the building," said Michael Kasperzak, a former Mountain View mayor who worked on the legislation. "If we have all these restaurants, we want this to be a successful development. If employers pay for it, that's fine." (Lee and Li 2018)

This is an excellent example of insider/outsider eating—not just metaphorically, but literally and physically—the employees inside the offices that never leave and the local community outside the office. The tech industry and its food programs have unintended consequences on those outside the industry. The policies of promoting commensality, generating new ideas, and keeping employees in the office longer are challenged here by the only institution that has the ability to force their hand—government.

But will laws actually change behaviors? When asked if they'd rather have more salary or free food, most respondents told me that they would rather have free food. In California, the response was even clearer among engineers, whose salaries were already high. An extra few thousand dollars a year made little difference to them and their bottom line. As Martin at Company A told me, "I'd rather have the convenience over the money."

The Kitchen as Meeting Room

An unused kitchen can be useful. At 10:15 a.m. at Company A, London, the kitchen was the social hub of the office. Tea, coffee, late breakfasts were all being made, past weekend plans were being discussed, and employees caught up about the week and what's happening. By 10:45 a.m., the kitchen table was being used as a meeting space. There were four employees having a meeting, for lack of an "official" meeting room—they were all booked.

The kitchen had multiple roles in the office space. It was an area that employees used to take a break and read their phones with a cup of coffee. It acted as a catchall—meetings, casual chats, eating, drinking—it was neutral. During my fieldwork I would sit in the kitchen with my notebook and a cup of coffee, waiting for employees to wander in—it was a good opportunity for casual conversations and for them to ask me some questions (like, "Are you still counting the number of cookies we eat?").

The kitchen didn't have a large enough table for all of the employees to eat at. There were only eight spaces, but thirty or so employees. In fact, during the Thanksgiving meal, tables were pushed together to form a long one that everyone could sit at. The first hurdle to getting employees to eat together is giving them the space to do so. A lack of space and this forces employees to take their food back to their desks,[2] go out to eat, or not eat at all. The weather in London rarely cooperated with the idea of eating outside in the park in front of the office but, when it did, employees told me they took advantage of it by bringing their food out to a bench or sitting on the grass with colleagues.

When the office was outfitted, the kitchen and eating spaces were constrained by budget and physical space. For example, Company A couldn't build a full kitchen because there weren't the correct utility lines available, and the building's owners wouldn't allow it. Although Kim told me that the kitchen and eating spaces were mentioned in the meetings leading up to the design choices, overall, it didn't take precedence. I'm not surprised.

There was a constant tug of war between philosophies and departments in these offices. Those who worked with and managed food programs were tasked with providing spaces for employees to gather and eat free meals. This was in tension with budgets and physical space constraints. Some employees would have preferred to have more meeting rooms, lounge spaces, or beanbag corners as opposed to more dining tables, and sometimes those employees had won the tug of war. All of the different spaces are important to the tech office, but the competing priorities meant that some offices didn't have the space required to instill the community-like, commensality-producing priorities that the organization had in mind.

We can use the phrase from Bauccio: "You are what your employees eat." Or put another way, companies are what they give their employees to eat; some argue you can actually chart some companies' successes and failures in the tech industry by the quality, quantity, and frequency of food and drinks (Pina e Cunha et al. 2008, 938).

I observed a number of tensions between the shared food spaces and culturally bound foodways inside the offices. At Company A, on days when there was no lunch provided, a couple of employees would bring some food from home to eat. Maria, in particular, was very passionate about cooking and would often be seen eating some leftovers from her dinner the previous evening. One afternoon, just past 1 p.m., she warmed up some fish in the microwave. The kitchen was not sealed off from the rest of the office space so if a staff member burned toast or heated up something particularly pungent, the entire office could smell it. This normally wasn't an issue—everyone's burnt a piece of toast at one point or another—but that day Maria's fish lunch drew in a number of really interesting, passive-aggressive assertions of how to use (and not use) shared spaces and the appropriateness of individual food choices.

From my desk, I overheard about six employees walk past the kitchen (individually) and say something along the lines of "That smells terrible!" There were also about five employees who said, "That smells great!" Maria didn't react to any of the comments but just kept eating her lunch, quietly, by herself. No one joined her at the kitchen table, perhaps put off by the smell.

A few minutes later, Karen came into the kitchen to make some toast. She covered it with a thick layer of Nutella, the chocolate hazelnut spread, placed it onto a paper plate, and walked back to her desk. The toast wasn't burnt yet the smell of toasted bread did fill the office for a brief period of time. No one made any mention of it.

Maria's choice of fish and Karen's choice of Nutella toast are perhaps representative of their respective cultural backgrounds—Polish and English. Maria displayed, throughout my time in the office, a penchant for cooking, and an understanding of foodways and dining out—she was a culinary explorer whose time in different countries had given her a palate for a number of more refined and exotic tastes. Karen's lunch was an excellent example of an English person and their apparent ambivalence toward cooking and cuisine. As Kate Fox mentions about the English, they don't have an inborn love of food like Europeans, and "food is not given the same high priority in English life as it is elsewhere" (Fox 2004, 296).

But even toast has more social connotations in the United Kingdom than Maria's fish dish. Toast, like tea, is the all-purpose, anytime comfort food. Fox tells us that what "tea alone does not cure, tea and toast surely will" (Fox 2004, 311–12). I can't claim to know if Karen was trying to deal with anything at all by eating Nutella toast, but the toast and tea trick was one that I found over and over again in both offices in London and Dublin.

But what does all of this talk about tea and toast and fish have to do with the shared spaces of cultural importance to each employee? The kitchen can really be thought of as the heart of the home and office and, to that extent, we can tend to bring our own emotions into the kitchen when things at work have become difficult or challenging. Tea and toast are emotionally linked in the English culture to feelings of awkwardness or being uncomfortable in a social situation. In other offices in the United States, tea and toast have little to no significance in the office or with emotional well-being. Since Fox doesn't mention gender in relation to tea and toast in the English culture, I have to assume that both genders use it for the reasons she explains.[3] Counihan also mentions the link between food and emotions in Florentine culture, noting that "the use of food to express and calm emotions was both dangerous and salutary" (Counihan 2004, 29): dangerous because of the potential for weight gain, but salutary because it helps one deal with difficult situations.

The shared spaces in these kitchens are ripe for more research into cross-cultural interactions related to sensorial aspects of food production and consumption. Nutella toast might appeal to the English, an Italian might be seen eating it for different reasons, but somehow both could be linked to an idea of home and comfort. Like our homes though, dishes can be left for the next day, for your partner to take care of, for the cleaning lady to manage.

Dirty dishes are piled in the sinks. Old food boxes litter the tables. It's past lunch and the kitchen remains a mess. There is not a lot of care that is taken in keeping the space clean and tidy. None of the passive-aggressive notes often found in offices to keep the kitchen clean or pick up after yourself. It's really different than other offices I've worked in where the kitchen "mother's not here" reminder notes are ubiquitous. Here, all the plates, cups, silverware are left for the cleaning lady to deal with in the afternoon. Why? Is this a cultural trait of the English who are used to leaving their used food trays and cups for others to clean up, like in the cafes and restaurants? (Field notes, Company A, London, December 2016)

Figure 5.3.   Company B dining areas in (L to R) Dublin, San Francisco, London.

Company B's Dining Room Example

You need appropriate physical space in order to be commensal.

Company B's dining areas stand out as exceptions in the tech industry. In each Company B office I visited (San Francisco, Dublin, and London), the space was designed with a communal table and dining area in mind. In London, space was bright, open, and welcoming. There was much more table space than there were employees; everyone had room to breathe.

In Dublin, the kitchen and dining room were on the top floor, complete with a small herb garden. It doubled as a yoga studio sometimes, and again, there was more space than was necessary given the number of employees. But the most important part of these spaces was that by far the majority of employees stopped what they were working on at lunchtime and filed into the dining room to eat. Here, finally, was a food program that was seemingly achieving its goals of getting people to take a lunch break, eat together, talk amongst the teams, and have a nutritious lunch. Here was a food program to use as a model. And the reason why I think Company B's program worked so well? The space. Space matters. Company B understands this; if you want employees to eat together, then you need space. Perhaps this is one reason why so many of the large tech companies in Silicon Valley started to bring food to employees in the first place—space. Building their "campuses" far away from any commercial center where there might be cafes and restaurants within walking distance, the office cafeteria became the center of the daily lunch break. Bringing it down to basic terms, Company B's spaces were designed with communal eating in mind. Where employees eat helps us understand the day-to-day social patterns of their working life as well as how space affects their rituals and habits (Strangleman 2010, 263).

The dining areas at Company B felt inclusive because the kitchen areas were clearly defined by walls or doors. They were decorated with murals in

London and in Dublin. In San Francisco, the walls were covered with artifacts from the Company B website, bought directly from some of their clients; it was a way to not only decorate an office but also highlight the diversity of items you could buy from their store. Company B had one up on Company A's spaces. Company A, without selling anything physical besides tickets for events, had little on their walls in way of decorations. In London, a neon sign on one wall announced the name of the company, but apart from that the walls were white, sparse, and clinical. The geography of the workspace is just as important to employees' well-being as the food that is served, but the geography of the workplace is usually neglected in many academic investigations.

There seemed to me to be a sense of freedom in the spaces I observed. In some cases, this was because of the size of the office, like Company A's office in San Francisco. There, you could easily spend your day avoiding those that you don't want to interact with by booking meeting rooms for yourself or simply by moving around the office and utilizing open spaces like sofas or the dining area. Employees were generally given freedom in the office that doesn't exist in other industries—and expected not to be micromanaged as a result.

Gershon points out that when you consider yourself to be some form of property—renting yourself out to an employer—you give up some of your freedom to do whatever you want during the day in return for some security (Gershon 2017, 13). That security is bound up inside the sense of freedom that people have. I believe that the sense of freedom has more to do with the fact that individuals feel free to leave jobs whenever they like and has less to do with the freedom within the office itself because, so many of the jobs, the employees I spoke with were expected to be, as Gregg says, always available and willing to respond to workplace demands (Gregg 2013, 154). This follows what is usually called an "agile" way of working, which demands that employees be flexible, respond to changes (instead of following a plan), and realize that technology changes quickly, so employees must keep up. While Gershon and Gregg generally don't discuss agility in their analysis of the workplace, Moore uses agility to better understand the ways in which these offices fit within a notion of a neo-Taylorian workplace. She says: "'Agile' has been appropriated into main-stream management terminology and job descriptions, even though it is unpopular with workers precisely because it breeds uncertainty" (Moore 2018, 44). While these are important aspects to consider when viewing office spaces like Company B's and Company A's, where agility is seen as a key way of working, it also fits into my own analysis that there is a sense of freedom in working in an agile environment that I believe Moore leaves out. An agile workforce is not micromanaged.

I never discovered the kinds of "updated Taylorism" that Moore chronicled. These kinds of tracking technologies, I believe, are designed for corporations and offices where the kind of agile working environment hasn't taken hold or is slow to be introduced. I find her negative outlook for the future of worker welfare and her assertions of intense surveillance overblown and difficult to relate to the offices I researched. That said, though, I agree with her assessment that neoliberalism is not that monster in the room, but it is rather "systematic effects of a particular labor process" which are portrayed in terms of employees' problems in adapting, psychological shortcomings, or lack of education in a bad way (Moore 2018, 55–56).

Lunch at Google—Round Two

Lanchester is right when he says that "plenty of companies, indeed entire industries, base their business model on being evil" (Lanchester 2017). The utopian mission statements of tech industries set a different model: these are overwhelmingly aimed at making the world a better place in some way. The freedom that employees are allowed to have in tech offices is both good for recruitment and also bad for maintaining a company culture consistent with these utopian aims.

It's hard to think that Google is evil when you're standing in one of their office canteens on the fifteenth floor of a skyscraper in Central London looking at a buffet of sushi. On an invitation to their London office by a friend of a friend, the idea of space and surveillance really came into view—this was the second investigative lunch at Google during my fieldwork. From the thoroughly marbled lobby (which was beautiful) to the bright and open, floor-to-ceiling glass windows surrounding it, it drips in excess and luxury. Google shared this building with a number of other companies, including a TV and entertainment firm. Employees entering the building, swiping their passes, and hitting the elevators' call buttons, were dressed impeccably. Yet there was a contingent who were also wearing trendy sneakers, T-shirts, and jackets—"the Googlers," I wrote down in my notebook. This was my second lunch at a Google office, after the first one in Sydney. I was greeted over an hour late by my host—let's call her Michelle—who showed up dressed as if she worked in a high-end legal office: high heels, an elegant business suit with earrings, madeup hair and makeup. She was in her early fifties. I remember thinking that employees like her skewed my data on what tech employees wear to work in general. I make note of this because, from other experiences at Google, it was unusual.

Despite her lateness, we had time for a quick tour of the two dining areas. Since I was not officially doing research at Google, these impromptu lunches were a great way to compare the offices of Company A and Company B with the "mothership" of Google. She told me that just six months ago, one of the cafes used to be entirely for those employees who had "free-from diets"—gluten, dairy, soy, carbs, sugar, and so on. "But they replaced it not long ago with an all-Asian food café—there were a lot of complaints," she said. Between the two canteens, they served over one thousand people. The space was immense, busy, hectic—employees walked around with laptops and phones, engaged in digital communication as they moved through the line for food (always connected, just like Miriam in Sydney). And the food! There was sushi, sashimi, pizza from a wood-fired oven, burgers, a salad bar, a smoothie bar, and several drinks fridges. This was really nothing new, but the quality was overwhelming.

We sat down, me with my sushi and a large salad, her with a smoothie. "The food is better in New York," she started out. "They have the best food of any Google office." I took note of this—she only had a few minutes and encouraged me to go get some dessert before it was all gone. "The pastry chef here is amazing—they come up with some really delicious and elegant things." She watched my half-eaten lunch while I walked over to the pastry counter, which resembled the one in Fortnum and Mason's department store in Piccadilly Circus. I chose two pastries and walked them back. "Good choice, the chocolate one is my favorite."

I could sense her unease with the situation, with what we were doing there, and so I asked her a few quick questions before she needed to go. Her responses were quick and to the point: "Google culture is stronger than local culture—lots of people eat at their desks, they are busy. In Southern Europe, they don't eat at their desks as much and tend to take around thirty minutes for lunch; in London, it's more like ten minutes or so. The free food," she continues, "saves the employees money, but yes, it does keep them in the office longer. It's really up to you to manage and balance your work and life—no one will tell you how to do that, or to do it at all. You have to balance your workday accordingly." Her thoughts about time management are supported by Gregg's work, who says that organizations are no longer responsible for coordinating time: "The injunction to use time resourcefully now falls on everyone" (Gregg 2018, 130).

In such a short moment, she summed up so much. Essentially, she is saying it's up to you, the employee, to leave on time. No one tells you to stay. She's the first person I talked to at any of these companies who explicitly said this.

I scarfed down my food so she could get back to work—I couldn't just hang around, I had to be escorted back down to the ground floor, and I felt like I had been intruding. I thanked her, said goodbye, and took a seat in the lobby to record my impressions and write down my notes. It solidified ideas about space and place—where employees appear to be trapped by busyness, not just the physical space of the office. This goes directly against the ideas about feeding employees in Silicon Valley, where offices were sometimes (and still are) located far away from town centers or commercial areas so employees had to get in their cars to leave for lunch. Bringing the food to them solved this. But in comparison, in this particular office space in London, there was so much food available just outside the doorstep that this argument only made sense thinking about employee well-being and fairness, as well as the ever-present idea of productivity. The big question that I have that is not answered here is, how productive can you be if you only take ten minutes to eat your lunch?

From an ethnographic standpoint, there were a number of interactions I had in these offices which tell a broader story about the culture of free food and how it differs from office to office. Michelle's comments at Google in London, even if brief, told one story. Miriam's at Google in Sydney told another. My own experience as a "worker" in these spaces, eating the same food and having access to the same snacks and drinks, gave me the perspective of what it meant to be an employee and be presented always with the same choices. I was allowed to eat as if I was an employee; I got access to snacks, drinks, and meals like any other. I accepted these food rituals as my own. This came to a head in the London Company A office, where I became very tired of the same kinds of meals.

My field notes show my own personal frustration with the lunches in the office and also some of the more humorous interactions I had with a few of the employees there about the meals. What these interactions reveal is the great range of conceptualizations of a meal, or of a cuisine. Here is a scene from a day at Company A, directly from my field notes.

Salad Box Frustration and Excess Food

Another round of salad boxes was being delivered for lunch one day. I took a picture and sent it to my wife.

I cannot eat another salad box.

My wife: What the hell is that?

It's a variation on a theme at Company A and after we talk a bit more about it, I've come to realize that the lunch box here is just an extension of the food that Kim, the office manager, likes to eat.

"All these boxes have too much protein," I wrote. "Why is there all of the mixed protein boxes? It feels excessive and not overly healthy actually, which is strange because it's meant to be healthy or at least, that is the common pre-conception."

Figure 5.4. Three of many salad boxes at Company A's London office

The next day we get lunch, it's "Mexican food." Christopher and I are both eating at our desk. He's reading the BBC news while he eats. "I've not eaten much Mexican food," Christopher says to me as he points to something in his lunch box resembling a blue corn tortilla. "What's this?" he asks. "That's a tortilla, it's a taco," I responded. "Oh, right, it's good."

It was not good, nor was it a real taco, but I ate it. It was combined with quinoa and some chickpeas—too much protein, I thought. Whoever thinks quinoa goes in a tortilla has obviously never been to Mexico. "I thought this was meant to be the unhealthy day," says Mike from the kitchen.

The tacos apparently didn't look unhealthy enough for him. Kim says it was the day before, actually, and he gets annoyed that he missed it. "I'm going out for some lunch, then."

This isn't an uncommon occurrence, actually. Mike has a fairly particular way of eating that I can't quite figure out but, on the surface, it appears to be a burgers and fries kind of diet: simple, unfussy. (Field notes, Company A, London, March 2017)

These notes are just a small example of the negative feedback Kim had to manage in the office. But from my notes you can see I got particularly upset or frustrated at the food too. Was I too becoming entitled? Later in the day, I took the opportunity to informally ask Kim a few questions about the lunches.

Int: Does the weather have an effect on what is ordered?

Kim: No, because the meal plan is put into effect at the beginning of the month.

Int: Is the food seasonal?

Kim: I'm not sure, really.

Int: Is it healthy?

Kim didn't really have an answer, because one day is certified as a "cheat day," lingo taken directly from a diet app or blog. The account manager at City Pantry, a company that helps offices manage their employees' food orders, is in charge of helping plan the meals according to the specifications that the company gives them. But these specifications don't come from the head office, necessarily.

> *Kim:* There is no program that is handed down from the head office. It is really up to each office to work it out for themselves.

> *Int:* Do people like the food?

> *Kim:* Yes and no. But mostly yes, they do. Although this past week there seemed to be a lot of leftovers, and it is hard to know if that is because people don't like what is being offered, or because there are a lot of people out of the office. A mixture, I assume.

> *Int:* What about not having enough room at the kitchen table for everyone to eat at?

> *Kim:* Sometimes people eat at their desks, and sometimes, you will find a lot of people eating together all at the same time.

During my observation, it was rare to see a lot of people eating together, and when it did happen it tended to be in the months leading up to Christmas. There was no clear community built around lunch, as it was intended, but rather there were casual opportunities to talk and share with each other.

On another day, the smell of warmed up gyros filters throughout the office. Gyros were one of the meals that employees there went crazy for. They were really good and came with excellent, skin-on fries. You could taste a hint of spice, perhaps cumin, a bit of mint, and an overwhelming amount of meat. Slowly, employees found their way to the leftovers from lunch, piled on the far table in the kitchen. One by one, the microwave came to life, throwing out scents of Greek food, delivered by scooter, ordered by one company, who told the restaurants how many, of what, for whom.

On another day, the afternoon snack session started with Maria cutting open a mango and an apple for an afternoon fruit salad, which seemed innocent enough but soon turned into her offering Nick, from marketing, half of a warmed-up wrap left from lunch. It was 3:45 p.m., snack time. Nick gladly accepted Maria's offer, and both returned to their desks with their food, spreading the scent throughout the office for all of us to smell. I found that even I was strangely drawn back to the kitchen, but resisted the afternoon "nosh," in lieu of an early dinner. Maria, it turned out, was in the kitchen often. Heating up food like the fish lunch, or cutting up some fruit, making coffee, having a snack.

Excess food was not a huge problem in an office full of young people who were all quite active (or so they said and appeared) as well as having me, one extra mouth to feed, and the cleaning lady, who gladly accepted anything

Figure 5.5. Lunch from "Hungry Donkey—Greek Kitchen"—Company A, London office.

that was offered to her for lunch as well. Waste was managed on a day-by-day basis, depending on a number of factors, like how much there was, what type of food it was, and what people would take home with them at the end of the day.

Nick once said to me, "We had a Christmas two years ago when there were only six people in the office, but food was ordered for thirty, so we took the leftovers to a homeless shelter at King's Cross." Having access to outlets to donate food seemed to be more of a challenge in London than in San Francisco. Company A's London office had meals delivered in single-serving boxes. These were difficult to donate and either got eaten, taken home, or thrown away. A few were saved for the days when meals were not provided, but fridge space was limited. At Company B's London office, leftovers were put away in the fridge for employees to eat and at the end of the week, anything left was donated to homeless shelters. It was easier because the meals at Company B were not individually packaged—they were served family-style. Similarly, at Company A in San Francisco, food was packaged for employees to eat when they wanted or to take home. Anything left at the end of the week was donated. Waste management was a big deal for these companies and one of the other tasks that the food program managers had on their plate. Working with local shelters was one approach, donation was another, and in San

Francisco there were, oddly enough, startups that dealt directly with sorting through donated food and getting it to the right place.

The company that Company B used was called Copia.[4] Their tagline is "Hunger Isn't a Scarcity Problem. It's a Logistics Problem." The basics of their approach were that businesses donate leftover food by scheduling a pickup time on the app. Copia collected all types of "edible surplus," as they called it, including highly perishable prepared foods. Drivers collected the food and were matched with the closest nonprofit to deliver it. These non-profits, who were also using the platform, create profiles to communicate the kind and quantity of food they need and when. It was a for-profit company that was connected to nonprofit groups. They charged a weekly fee of $15 USD, which allowed Company B to donate between five and twelve pounds of leftover food.

Compared to Nick's account of taking the food themselves to the homeless shelter at King's Cross, Copia relieves companies from officially having to deal with the oftentimes difficult task of finding out where to donate food. Food waste is part of the picture, and an area for future research.

NOTES

1. Actually, I found it difficult to focus at times because of the amount of noise. The music playing or the number of people walking around on their phones (this was especially true in the Company A, London office) was distracting. But counter to that, I found the Company B office in London to be eerily quiet, almost too quiet.

2. There is a hashtag on social media for #saddesklunch.

3. Fox says that actually "tea is still believed, by English people of all classes, to have miraculous properties. A cup of tea can cure, or at least significantly alleviate, almost all minor physical ailments and indispositions, from a headache to a scraped knee. Tea is also an essential remedy for all social and psychological ills, from a bruised ego to the trauma of a divorce or bereavement. This magical drink can be used equally effectively as a sedative or a stimulant, to calm and soothe or to revive and invigorate."

4. http://gocopia.com.

Chapter Six

Commensality at Work

COMMENSALITY RE-HASHED

Commensality is the concept used to describe eating with others—literally eating at the same table (*mensa*) (Kerner et al. 2015, 12). While it needs little introduction here, it is an important concept to mention because it grounds my research. Where many academics (Hochschild 1997, Scholliers 2001, Andersen et al. 2015) draw the conclusion that not many employees are eating meals together at work or, as Sobal says, in "institutional commensal units," what my research shows is that this is not necessarily true across the board (Sobal and Nelson 2003, 181). While it may have been true when those studies took place, my ethnographic research shows that inside Company A and Company B the institutional commensal unit is in fact being supported by the company itself. Sobal goes on to suggest that breakfast is the meal most likely eaten alone. I would agree with that assessment based on my findings. Breakfast, even if had in the office, was usually eaten alone, at the employees' desk or workstation—my own included.

Commensality can be thought about structurally, in terms of commensal units and commensal circles. These shape and create our social worlds. We know that commensal units are "groups of people assembled at a particular time and specific place to consume meals, snacks, or beverages. The family is the most fundamental commensal unit, although others include work groups on lunch breaks, friends eating together at a restaurant, neighbors sharing a beverage as they chat over the fence and other types of eating partners" (Sobal and Nelson 2003, 181). While this view might be aspirational and based on a number of "powerful coalition of forces and agents [that] have come together to make the family meal a part of the cultural politics"

(Wilk 2010, 428), what I believe, based on my own investigation, is that the most fundamental commensal unit for many people is the work group. The research on commensality at work, from the past,[1] doesn't seem to even consider the idea that more meals might now be served at work. And indeed, as Wilk notes, "when we assume that happy family meals are normal, anything else tends to become invisible, or if seen, interpreted as deviance or evidence of social decay" (Wilk 2010, 430). Yet I could not find in my own research anything that seemed to corroborate this on a large scale. Sure, there were the exceptions; consider the tales of Miriam, Sandra, or Michelle, who rarely shopped for themselves or cooked at home. This doesn't necessarily place them into a category of a deviant, but it does place them into a category of people who, for one reason or another, are not part of a strong commensal unit outside of work.

To wrap up this thought perfectly, Wilk says that "while eating does seem to be a universal form of social life in every society anthropologists have studied, the nuclear family is not the unit of commensality in a majority of cases. Instead, the majority of the world's people eat together in age grades, in gender-segregated non-family groups, and in family groups both smaller and larger than nuclear families" (Wilk 2010, 430). It is really about understanding how commensal circles are developed through inclusion or exclusion in various commensal units. They are "networks of relationships that delineate the range of people whom individuals could, have, and do eat with" of which families, claims Sobal (Sobal and Nelson 2003), still form the core of most commensal circles.

In tech offices with young, mostly single workers, the idea of eating with your family might actually be eating in non-family groups. In more "senior" tech companies like Google or Adobe, where employees might skew older, eating with your family becomes more pronounced. Even Martin, at Company A, mentioned this in my interview with him, where he talked about how food perks shift in their importance as one ages and advances in life.

Both cultural values and structural individualism offer ways to understand commensal patterns. The cultural values perspective places a focus on the cultural norms and societal pressure to eat together. It suggests the idea that a proper or ideal meal must be eaten together and eating alone isn't considered to be a real meal (Douglas 1972, Fischler 1980, Sobal and Nelson 2003).

The structural individualism approach focuses, instead, on the effects of "social isolation and the fast pace of mass society in a post-industrial era as a hindrance to commensal eating" (Sobal and Nelson 2003, 182), or what Fischler says is eating without others who provide social support or outside of established rules of cuisine (Fischler 1980, 948). What I argue is that tech companies are actively working against the idea of the structural individualistic approach to commensality, whether or not they set out to do so. They are actively trying to alter the very things that many of their products have worked to create; the entire concept of being more isolated while being more connected digitally works against the idea of commensality. Rectifying this inside the companies by providing meals is one way to help employees regain the social support structures they need in order to live. The cultural values theory has some basis here as well, but it is less developed in the tech company because it relies more on the idea that society implies that eating together is the rule. But not all societies work this way, and even North American and Western European societies are shifting more toward the individualist approach. We see this in Ho's account of eating in the financial industry, where she discusses taking too much time in the cafeteria or not taking your meal back to your desk. Busyness trumps any societal pressure to eat together.

> In fact, many of the front-office floors featured their own "express cafés," where only the brown cardboard boxes were available, as everyone was expected to buy lunch and bring it back to their desks to continue work. (Ho 2009, 121)

The concept of commensality is widely covered in a range of disciplines, articles, books, and even magazines, blogs, and Instagram posts, which I think offer a unique way of understanding how people interpret the idea today. Logging onto Instagram, the first post that uses the hashtag is from @joryclay, who posted an image of the Thanksgiving meal at their home and used the hashtag #commensality under it. Following that, @africanfoodrevolution posted an image of a meal with no caption; it simply had the hashtags #commensality and #africanfoodrevolution. Further down, I found @cribs4u, whose images of a family reunion was a great reflection of commensality. The hashtags they used were #commensality and #familyreunion.

> The dining space in the San Francisco office [of Company A] feels like a school hall. (Johnny, Company A employee in London)

I was at my desk at Company B's London office. It was pouring rain outside, and I was working on some field notes. At one o'clock on the dot, the lunch bell was rung, and the food manager yelled out "LUNCH." I waited at my desk to watch, in sync, how the employees stopped what they were doing and filed into the kitchen, where an array of salads, light dishes, and food had been arranged on the counter. Real plates, silverware, and glasses were set at long wooden tables that seated around eight on a side. It reminded me repeatedly of my high school cafeteria. From the lunch bell to the long tables, from the orderly line and the timing—it all felt very school-like. Cheryl, one of the staff members, put it this way:

> Obviously, not everybody gets along with everybody, and we still try to . . . I know it's bad, actually, but we try to sit with a person you actually want to speak to or across from this person. Sometimes you can see some awkward movements where people are like, "Hmm, how can I do this without sitting next to this person?" I don't think it necessarily . . . It's still nice to sit across the person you get along with or I speak to, but I don't think the feeling of community really applies with everybody. It's not like this has to work so that magic can happen all the time and people . . . Sometimes there's just nothing to talk about. Without even some drama, I just mean, literally, there's no interests or nothing in common and you just sit there awkwardly.

Schools hold strong memories for many people. If I think back to high school, a lot of the food did not seem made for high productivity. Much of it made me terrible sleepy in the afternoon. It was food made to fill the bellies of hungry students—it wasn't meant to be a way to entice them to come to school, to spend more time there, or to be productive. But food also works to divide people—and high school is the perfect example, where cliques form, you know who to eat with, where to sit, and so on. This happens in tech companies as well—new employees (or a visiting researcher) have to force their way into a group, ask to sit at a table, and find a crowd. Even in smaller offices I visited, there were avoidances. Some employees didn't like to eat with certain other employees and obvious cliques formed, reminding us that commensality can also promote conflict (Bove et al. 2003, 33).

Schools are not the only institutions that resembled these office spaces. Hospitals also have much to share with corporate dining spaces. Not known for having great food generally, hospitals do provide meals based on their needs and conditions. Tech companies have created a system of care that also caters to individual dietary need (or in their case, sometimes catering to individual wants). In trying to please elite (even entitled) employees, companies often appeal to individual food requirements. It could be vegetarian, vegan, or gluten-free. Or it could be a demand for "cheat days" and junk food. Maybe it is a personal choice or a religious-based restriction. Whatever it is, customization is actually expected.

Attesting to this, Charlotte at Company A in San Francisco told me about a time when a vegan employee was outraged at her for the lack of vegan choices at lunch. There was always at least one dish that was vegan, as well as a salad bar, but that wasn't enough for this employee, who complained of having to buy her own meals during the week. In general, though, the unwritten rule of these companies was that if there is free food provided, you eat it. The urge to eat what is given to you instead of going out for lunch was strong.

I might be claiming that this is forced commensality, and those who study meals in prisons might object to the comparison. But just like in a prison, tech company employees are more or less held hostage, especially if and when the location of the office is far from any commercial center, workers lack time to go out for lunch, there is peer pressure to eat in the office, or, as one person reported, there is a fear of leaving the office because of the people on the street. The reasons are different, but the result is the same. The food is arguably better in the tech offices than prisons but could still be used for behavior control. Jones refers to two crucial factors that differentiate most "penal policies, procedures, and provisions from those related to food served in the military, school lunch programs, college dorms, and hospitals." In his formulation,

> that is, food in prison is used to manipulate people, alter behavior, and force inmates to conform to the alleged needs of the system. The second major difference between penal provisioning and food in non-punitive settings is that in many prisons the food is—whether by design, neglect, or indifference—part of the punishment. (Jones 2017, 73)

This is an important point. Food does have the ability to change behavior and it can be used to control people. Those people could be in prison or an office. How different is it that companies, like Company A and Company B, use food as a way to gather employees together? Or as a tool to keep them in the office longer? Is that not food being used as a behavior control method? It is indirect, but effective nonetheless. Charlotte told me during one of our interviews that "the more things you provide on-site, the longer people stay at work and hang out and some keep working. I think that's why the big campuses, you're like, oh you don't actually have to leave."

I can't say I noticed any instances where food was used as a punishment— or the lack of food was used in this way, although I am sure some employee complaints about the type of food, the lack of certain snacks, or the empty shelves of a LaCroix on a Friday afternoon might count in their minds as a punishment. It has been noted that some prisons deny culturally suitable meals, withhold meals, serve rotten food, or oftentimes prepare meals that lack spices, salt, or pepper (as forms of control or punishment). Tech companies, on the whole, cater to almost any personal choice or cultural need that exists (Jones 2017, 78). Perspective is everything, yet still food is a symbol of institutional power and control.

There is an interesting dichotomy here to think about prisoners eating in a large mess hall and at restaurants. David Beriss tells us that using the concept of commensality to frame eating in a restaurant is wrong because "when we eat in restaurants, we don't share food with all the people in the restaurant. At least, not since the invention of modern restaurants in the late eighteenth century. Usually, you sit down and order your own meal from a menu. You might share with the people at your table and if commensality is going to be invoked, it is there that you will find it" (Beriss 2018). Commensality needs, for it to work, sharing with friends, family, people around you. When Jones talks about prisons, there is no mention of sharing, friends, or family. So ideally, commensality, at least if we use Beriss's concept, is sharing. This turns the entire idea of eating at work, in a tech office, a bit askew—especially in offices where individually portioned meals are provided and differentiated according to individual dietary preferences. These are apt to be eaten alone, at the desk, avoiding any notion definition of commensality.

In her book about Florentine families, Counihan addresses the idea that the table is the place where family problems are worked out. She says that "several of my subjects reported tense meal interactions" (Counihan 2004, 116). This is exactly what prisons (and, to some extent, offices and schools) are not trying to encourage—commensality in the family sense, in the Italian sense, is different than elsewhere. Later in the same chapter, Rinaldo says:

> Sometimes my wife and I have arguments at dinner. We bring our problems to the dinner table. If we have an argument in the morning, we avoid each other during the day. . . . It happens at dinner that we go back to the arguments. (Counihan 2004, 118)

The table is a place to share concerns, argue, and talk about money, health, and life's woes in general. While employees at Company B and Company A didn't share medical issues or financial problems or argue about politics at the table, the dining table at home might be different. The dining table at home is also not a place, as Counihan reports, for strangers. I think that this idea holds true today, where strangers are not usually welcomed inside houses to share a meal with others. We don't welcome strangers to sit at our table in a restaurant (apart from restaurants that have large communal tables, such as Le Pain Quotidien) and, in general, it is relatives, friends and those closest to us that we prefer to dine with. Dining with strangers is something I relate to eating a meal on an airplane—you are more or less forced to do it. Yet, the topics of conversation at the tables that I sat at usually focused on topics unrelated to work, for the most part. Movies, weather, holiday plans, what might be considered small talk, or chit-chat, or just "being nice." While there were certain employees who had more sustained and in-depth relationships with each other, and thus, most likely shared more personal details, at large tables where there is a sense of being in school, personal details were kept mostly at bay. This plays into the idea of the open office as well—you never know who is listening in.

Mess Halls and Forced Commensality

Looking to the past, communist mess halls in China during the Great Leap Forward provide a useful model for the understanding the idea of forced commensality in today's tech offices. Usually, elite groups try to mark themselves by eating special status or elite foods, but not in the tech industry. Party leaders, like tech company bosses, all share the same food access in the office. It is very egalitarian. There are those who work outside of the tech industry, though, who believe (and rightly so) that those who work in tech are already marking their high societal status by eating the free food, by not buying food from local cafes and restaurants, and by highlighting their "luck" on social media platforms.

No tech company would tell you that their employee policies resemble communist or socialist ideas. It has to be said though that there are more than a few overlaps. "At their extremes, capitalism and communism become equivalent," to borrow Martinez's phrase (Martinez 2016, 355). The underlining rule in the offices I investigated was that if the food was free and available, you ate it. Rarely did you venture out, according to Watson (2010) and Martinez (2016), to procure your own. Time is also of importance to both tech companies and collectively organized factories. Both groups sought out ways to save time so that it could be converted into productive labor—one way is to have food ready and prepared. Employees did not have to leave the office to eat (or in some cases, go to the gym, the doctor, have their hair done, change their car oil, etc.).

But protests also show up on occasion in the tech industry, especially when food comes into play. Each office that I was in had a formal feedback system in place online where employees could tell the food manager (or in London, the office manager) about the food that was served that day. More often than not, Kim in London just asked people face-to-face—which, in England, is not a sure way to get the most honest response.

Stories circulate about the ways in which employees at Google in Silicon Valley protested the choice to participate in "Meatless Mondays" by holding a protest barbecue in the parking lot, ransacked break rooms, threw forks, and wrote anonymous opinions online mentioning that they would get a job at "Microsoft, Twitter, or Facebook where they don't f*** with us" (Bock 2015, 322).

At Company A in London, management tended to eat together or at their desks, instead of with the non-managers. Even during Thanksgiving, the managers were grouped at one end of the table. In my analysis, this was a signal that they were in charge. This was an important moment to signal that leadership, because in an open office it is sometimes difficult to know who is in charge. The more standard signals, like having a corner office, being the best dressed, or being the oldest, were not there. Elsbach tells us "the size of an office, its location, the number of windows, and the quality of furnishings, for example, are commonly used as indicators of organizational rank, prestige, and status" (Elsbach 2004, 111). Yet, in every office I observed, none of these factors came into play in regard to the status of employees. Eating together was one way to solidify their solidarity as managers, as leaders, and to signal to others their place in the office.

Fischler supports the idea that long, rectangular tables with a prominent seat at one end or in the middle (as in the Last Supper) are more

> adapted to hierarchy and vertical commensality (one in which the attention of participants is focused on one leading character, as opposed to "horizontal" commensality with friendly, informal long tables). The physical space defined by the table shape is a social space and the arrangement of employees around it reflects their relationships and hierarchical structure. (Fischler 2011, 535)

Who's in Charge Here?

At Company A in San Francisco, it was difficult to visually understand who was in charge. Apart from the CEO, who had a very clearly defined space of her own, to my outsider's eye, managers were difficult to identify. The dining area wasn't divided, there weren't separate bathrooms, and there were no separate dining rooms for managers and non-managers. Some tables, although not all, were round, which Fischler says allows "maximum equality and exchanges between participants in the meal." King Arthur chose a round table so that none should have precedence. Round tables are well known for helping promote conversations but, then again, some cultures don't use tables at all. A table is just a tool that enables us to have a place to set our plates and glasses on—it keeps things hygienic, in some respects, by not using the floor, which we usually regard as being dirty. At my own university in Illinois, where I studied for my undergraduate years, the dining hall only had round tables. It was the first time I was presented with them in an institutional setting. Most schools, I would argue, use square or rectangular ones—which fit nicely into mostly square spaces. Round tables mean wasted space in restaurants (I didn't observe any round tables in the restaurants I went to), which, in the end, means less profit. Overall, round tables are less efficient when space is at a premium.

The social analyst Tim Strangleman analyzed dining room division in his research on the Guinness factory in London, where there were five dining rooms for different groups of workers, including the staff, foremen, senior managers, and directors; the differences though, were slim. Each was given a menu and was served with what he calls "silver service" by waitresses (many of whom were mothers, daughters, or wives of the men working in the brewery) (Strangleman 2010, 267). Strangleman's account of the Guinness factory, though, is very different from those of tech companies where hierarchy has been stripped back, silver service is unheard of, and, as Paolo Rossi of Company B told me, there is a strong motivation to "avoid the embedded division of service workers relative to physical space." Company B was aware that a division was going to eventually happen, and they were actively thinking about ways to avoid it. Ideas like rotating employees through as dishwashers were proposed, but in the end were difficult to implement and manage. How do you manage a roster of three hundred people? You need to create a new position just to control it. Bigger offices create "culture growth problems," as Paolo told me. It seems his main task was not just to manage the global food program, but to also act as a guide to how the work culture of Company B should grow. Unfortunately, Paolo's ideas were put to rest when the company made him redundant along with many of his food program colleagues. How the work culture of Company B continues to change is now in the hands of the employees themselves. Konnikova says:

> Though open offices often fostered a symbolic sense of organizational mission, making employees feel like part of a more laid-back, innovative enterprise, they were damaging to the workers' attention spans, productivity, creative thinking, and satisfaction. (Konnikova 2014)

The organizational mission is, at times, more important than workers' attention spans, productivity, creative thinking, and satisfaction. It seems that these companies were unable to think of the two as opposing, rather than enhancing each other. The company mission stands at the center of all things—and it's ironic to see that there is research to support the idea that the open office plan actually works against the ideas of creativity and idea generation. Some studies say that open office plans are popular because they are cheaper. That could be one reason, but I also think they are popular because it is easier to make them feel homey. "The goal was to have a place of business with the feel of someone's house, but under one roof," says a newspaper article from San Diego, talking about a firm's renovated office space (Hirsh 2012). The idea of home is creeping into the tech offices and it's becoming apparent that these spaces, though they are trying to imitate home as much as they can, are failing.

Responses to questions about work habits during my field interviews told me that employees were happy to work "from home" as much as they are allowed. Also, some companies promote working from home as a perk. If employees really thought of the office as home, then working from home would not be as important. So why is there so much emphasis placed on it? I think it has more to do with the distractions in the open office plan than anything else.

Brown reports that office workers lose three to five hours of productive work time a day due to interruptions—68 percent of which come from internal sources (Brown 2017). A study from 1982 by Hedge says that the most frequently cited disturbances are "other coworkers" instead of office machines (Hedge 1982). Office machines have probably gotten a lot quieter since 1982, and I am sure that this statistic holds true in the tech offices of today.

Is the open office at risk of attack like the free food programs? Perhaps there is a small but muted backlash beginning, but it is far from shifting back to a work arrangement of private offices and closed doors. More likely is a scenario, described as a "palette of places" (Lohr 2017). The newest models of office design call for largely open, but not completely open, spaces. Bringing people together is still thought of as being a positive attribute but so are team spaces, standing tables, comfortable couches, and movable walls. Most often looked over, it seems, is privacy. In the tech industry, where many employees require periods of intense concentration, the new ways of designing offices mean that employees have more places to seek out solitude than in the "neo-Dickensian" workbench arrangements. Some offices now include isolation rooms, soundproof rooms, and lounges where technology is forbidden (Lohr 2017).

Concentration is not just about escaping colleagues and phones, but music too. Oppressive music in these spaces is distracting—it was to me, and it is for employees who work there. The music in the Company A office in London was always on. It didn't seem like there was any option but to have music. The space was filled with noises. I noted previously the lack of music and noise at the Company B office in London. It was shocking coming from the very noisy Company A office, but also showed some kind of simple compassion, I think. Employees could choose to use headphones and listen to whatever they liked instead of having noise imposed on them.

We might wonder how commensality is linked to distraction and noise levels. Eating together can be noisy, something that I can attest to. Eating at Company A offices in both London and San Francisco were noisy affairs. Given that the office was open, it is a big distraction for workers. Some even felt pressure to eat because they could see that everyone was going to eat—that they were lining up. At Company B, this was less common. My experience in both London and San Francisco was that lunchtime was not a loud occasion. Again, space plays a big role in this.

All this is to bring out the point that sometimes, the concept of productivity is being pushed aside by the very practices that have been "designed" to promote it. What is helpful and productive for one employee might not be for another, and this brings us around to a discussion on labor.

NOTE

1. That is, apart from Strangleman's research on the Guinness factory in London, which is a surprisingly great account of commensality in a factory setting. Commensality in a factory setting, I feel, deserves more attention.

Chapter Seven

Labor

WILL WORK FOR FOOD

What is the value of work? It seems like a simple question but is surprisingly difficult to answer. Increasingly, work means producing things that don't physically exist—websites, content, apps, code—the tech industry is built upon this kind of work. It becomes increasingly difficult for companies to monitor output in these kinds of situations. Think about the car factory where there is a link between work and how many cars you made that day. You can see the results of your time. Meanwhile, in the tech industry, results are harder to see and even harder to feel fulfilled by.

To consider work in the tech industry, we first have to place it in the right context. Most tech companies' main products are not physical, but digital; they operate flat corporate structures, don't offer unions for employees, don't pay overtime, and usually have, what some might call, utopian ideas for what they want to achieve in the world. This section will utilize the theories put forth by David Harvey in his book where he analyzes the overview of the shift from "Fordism" to "flexible accumulation." He says:

> To begin with, the more flexible motion of capital emphasizes the new, the fleeting, the ephemeral, the fugitive, and the contingent in modern life, rather than the more solid values implanted under Fordism. (Harvey 1989, 171)

Using Harvey's analysis of political economy in relation to work and the shifts in labor since 1973, we can begin to see how the tech industry fits into "flexible accumulation" but also flexible work. You don't have to look only to the auto industry to see this shift. Within Silicon Valley, there has also been a move from the kind of companies that built the physical products

125

that computers and the internet rely on, to a more agile kind of industry. Those companies, like Intel for example, the maker of microchips, still exist, but even their modes of producing microchips have shifted to more robotic means of production. Shankar builds on this by saying that "Fordist mass production has been replaced by advanced capitalism, and the shift from product- to process-oriented economies has flourished in Silicon Valley" (Shankar 2008, 29).

Where did leisure go, though? Going back to Harvey, we can see where it used to be from his account of Fordism:

> Ford believed that the new kind of society could be built simply through the proper application of corporate power. The purpose of the five-dollar, eight-hour day was only in part to secure worker compliance with the discipline required to work the highly productive assembly-line system. It was coincidentally meant to provide workers with sufficient income and leisure time to consume the mass produced products the corporations were about to turn out in ever vaster quantities. (Harvey 1989, 126)

How is this different from tech companies trying to create new modes of working and commerce through corporate power? The corporate power that a company like Company A yields over employees is utilized in a way that almost tries to achieve the same things as Ford was trying to do, only without the hourly wage and the eight-hour day. But the consumption model has changed—while the salaries are high and workers at Company A might have the money to buy things, the idea of leisure time has been diminished in favor of a celebration of long office hours—which is where free food comes into play. Ford never had to provide workers with free food at the factory—this, I feel, would have been beyond his own ideas about how to support workers in ways that make financial sense and eating at home with the family was part of his ideas about the social lives of employees (Harvey 1989, 126). But at Company A and Company B, their workdays are flexible, the workers must be agile, and they are not paid on a per-piece basis—I think it is safe to say that the work is ambiguous at best.

Let's talk a bit more about flexible accumulation, though, because it has merit in this discussion of the tech industry as a whole. Harvey's definition of flexible accumulation is that it is

> marked by a direct confrontation with the rigidities of Fordism. It rests on flexibility with respect to labor processes, labor markets, products, and patterns of consumption. It is characterized by the emergence of entirely new sectors of production, new ways of providing financial services, new markets, and, above all, greatly intensified rates of commercial, technological, and organizational innovation. It has entrained rapid shifts in the patterning of uneven develop-

ment, both between sectors and between geographical regions, giving rise, for example, to a vast surge in so-called "service-sector" employment as well as to entirely new industrial ensembles in hitherto underdeveloped regions (such as the "Third Italy," Flanders, the various silicon valleys and glens, to say nothing of the vast profusion of activities in newly industrializing countries). It has also entailed a new round of what I shall call "time-space compression" in the capitalist world—the time horizons of both private and public decision-making have shrunk, while satellite communication and declining transport costs have made it increasingly possible to spread those decisions immediately over an ever wider and variegated space. (Harvey 1989, 147)

Here, he mentions directly "silicon valleys and glens" and is surprisingly accurate at how the world has developed given that it was written so long ago. Two key ideas are at play here, that work has become flexible and that the distinction between work and leisure has collapsed. Bringing this up to date, Pfeilstetter even mentions this in his account about the sociality of young male tech employees in Manchester (Pfeilstetter 2017, 8). Gershon uses the idea of personal branding to understand leisure activities, and, in this way, we can begin to also see the post-Fordist model in action even more. She suggests that a way for employees to market themselves in an unstable labor market is to use leisure activities or hobbies as a means of showing stability. The ironic part is some employees don't have time to take up a hobby or leisure activities and that employees might actually construct their brand around culturally acceptable hobbies so they can fashion an "image that will create a sense of coherence no matter how many career transitions the person might make (Gershon 2016, 236).

Over the months since I was in the field, Company B restructured twice, and Company A was preparing an IPO launch, which usually means shoring up finances and cutting costs where necessary. Many informants were made redundant or moved on to other companies in the short time since my fieldwork. One employee at Company B got sent back to the United States from London after being laid off as her visa was linked to her job. Some were the victims of changing priorities or financial straits in their company, but others left by choice, citing the mere boredom of the job itself to pursue their own "hobbies," which were their real passions (more on this in a moment).

Connecting this back to the idea of free food, my main point here is that the shift since 1973 toward a more flexible way of working has meant that the meal break at work has changed too. In many tech companies, taking a full lunch break is a sign of not pitching in enough. It resembles what Karen Ho talks about in her analysis of the finance industry where she tells us that going out to lunch or eating in the cafeteria were "activities one had to control strictly" and that being seen eating in the cafeteria too much or for too long was "not considered professional, except on occasion, because it connoted time away from hard work" (Ho 2009, 6).

Yet, while these companies want workers to be flexible in regards to their work, the food programs remained mostly inflexible in nature, for example, the desserts running out quickly, the scheduled eating times, the limited menus, the ringing of the lunch bell. These programs are really a revival of Fordism in a post-Fordist context. It would be more flexible for companies to offer other ways of getting free meals—corporate charge cards, using Uber Eats, Deliveroo, or JustEat delivery services for on-demand dining—but that would work against the value of commensality. You can't be endlessly flexible if you want people to come together around a common meal. There have to be set times and places for people to do this. It seems there is a nostalgia here for more of a "personal touch" that comes with non-flexibility rather than pure flexible accumulation.

I observed employees habitually working longer hours (or at least being physically in the office for longer periods of time) and skipping out on a full lunch hour. Most of them realized this was a trade-off between time and perks and they said it did not bother them. Companies provide opportunities and benefits that free employees from the drudgeries of domestic life. Lyons discusses unions fighting for better hours a century ago yet now tech employees celebrate their own exploitation and celebrate the idea that the hardship is part of the allure (Lyons 2017).

In January 2019, a *New York Times* article lamented the fact that so many young people are pulled into the idea of "performative workaholism" as a lifestyle (Griffith 2019). She really hits the nail on the head though, when she says about the tech employees she is surrounded by:

> In San Francisco, where I live, I've noticed that the concept of productivity has taken on an almost spiritual dimension. Techies here have internalized the idea—rooted in the Protestant work ethic—that work is not something you do to get what you want; the work itself is all. Therefore any life hack or company perk that optimizes their day, allowing them to fit in even more work, is not just desirable but inherently good. (Griffith 2019)

What she is talking about is really the "hustle culture." Basically, it means that to succeed you have to give up everything.[1] Yet, the ones beating the drums of "hustle mania" are at the top, who stand to financially profit the most. Dan Lyons writes about this mentality and calls it simply "thinking different," where companies are branding workaholism as a "desirable lifestyle choice" (Lyons 2017).

On some level, the practice of giving free food only helps to enhance feelings of busyness in the office. The "time poor" employee with free lunch builds that into their day—into their life. It contributes to a sense of busy that is pervasive in this industry. You must always feel or look busy. I too felt this in the office—not wanting to appear to be too idle because everyone else appeared to be busy. I took to walking around with my iPad or laptop, keeping the cup of coffee close by (to signal my busyness), typed frantically, and tried to fit in. Two employees told me during interviews about their experience joining these companies and learning that the laptop is not something you leave at your desk during a meeting. Amanda at Company B in London said:

> I've never worked in a job where having a laptop with you all the time is standard. I was used to coming to a meeting with my notebook—I prefer to write my notes down. I think the laptop prevents casual interactions before a meeting starts—there is less chitchat, less asking others how their day is going.

We might ask, then, why employees don't revolt and rise up against the cult of overwork. Unions, who might represent workers on these issues, are mostly non-existent in the tech industry (despite some movements toward it).[2] I heard repeatedly during my fieldwork that most employees in tech do not feel like they need protection. They have high wages, benefits, and what feels like a secure job—and it is all true except for the last part. None of the work is truly secure; it's all flexible. There are some indications though that workers are starting to realize their power. In November of 2018, about twenty thousand Google employees participated in a walkout, protesting the company's handling of sexual abuse claims. Others helped to shut down military contracts with the US government, showing the power that staff have in some areas. But I will point out, they have surprisingly little power in other areas that a traditional union would work to protect (work hours, benefits, overtime, pensions, etc.).

Employers are still shouldering a variety of risks for employees, but accompanying the changes is a new "ethos of market individualism" in the tech industry and Silicon Valley. Jacoby says:

> Believing that they must have a broad range of skills to succeed in today's labor market, these workers expect to spend no more than brief stints at any single firm. They ask only that the employer ensure their future employability by providing learning experiences that can be added to their resumes. Less concerned with job security than the generations who were touched by the Depression, they see themselves as masters of their own fates. They resemble nineteenth-century craft workers, who treasured their autonomy and hedged their labor-market risk with a diverse set of skills. (Jacoby 1999, 125)

Informant after informant confirmed this by telling me that they had been through several different jobs with starts and stops. Charlotte was once a ski lift manager in Vail, Colorado, before moving to the Bay Area for more opportunities. She also managed a LuLu Lemon shop. How these jobs are related to being the primary caregiver and food manager at Company A, I struggle to understand, apart from her abilities to provide customer service and manage spreadsheets.

PRODUCTIVITY

Business research tells us that employees will be more productive—and the sense of community at work and the company overall will benefit—if you give them free food and places to eat it (Bauccio 2013, Cappelli 2014, Bock 2015, Chance et al. 2016, Taylor 2017). But these concepts are built on economic theories instead of social theories. That is their major flaw. One way to conceptualize this is using Dunbar's Law, which suggests that there is a limit on the number of people that an individual can maintain stable social relationships with—150 is often cited as the highest number. Some companies have taken this to heart, like the Gore-Tex Company, who built office buildings that hold exactly 150 employees with parking lots that hold exactly 150 cars. When one building is full, they build a new one for 150 more employees (Gladwell 2013, 185). But this is extreme. Some tech companies prefer to have more people in closer spaces in order to promote the sharing of "knowledge and opinions," according to one study, which says that knowledge and opinions

> were most correlated among employees sharing an office, that correlations declined with distance for employees on the same floor of a building, and that employees on different floors of the same building were no more correlated than employees in different cities. (Cowgill et al. 2009, 2)

What this really says is that proximity is key to developing social relations between employees. So going back to the idea of business studies contributing toward the concept of productivity and building community as goals, what I argue is that employees are only as productive as they need to be, regardless of food benefits. If you take the food away, employees will still do the work they need to do so that they don't get in trouble. Productivity is difficult to measure, and everyone has a different idea about what it means, especially when it comes to knowledge workers (Palvalin et al., 2017, Óskarsdóttir and Oddsson, 2017, Moussa et al., 2017, Karr-Wisniewski and Lu, 2010).

Free food keeps people in the office longer, which, in turn, some might interpret as being productive. But as some employees told me sometimes you can get all your work done in a just a few hours, which means that you spend the rest of your time on Facebook, browsing the internet, online shopping, or pretending to be busy until it's time to go home. Granted, that was not the case for nearly all my informants, but for a few, like Kim, her work came in bits and pieces, leaving her time to attend acting auditions or maintain a blog. But it's more than this. It is a blurring of work and life where there is no real distinction between checking Facebook and personal email, because these are all felt to be urgent in some way—even if it is not the Fordist definition of work. It is busyness but not necessarily productiveness. It's what Gregg calls the "constant expectation of activity in the workplace that is facilitated through technology" (Gregg 2018). It's the example that Graeber gives in *Bullshit Jobs* of needing to pretend to be busy in the restaurant he was working in as a teenager, regardless of whether or not there was any real work to be done. In his words, he learned "if you're on the clock, do not be *too* efficient" because the result was that you would have to "pretend" to work, which was the most "absolute indignity" (Graeber 2018, 93).

The idea of bringing people together to share ideas is one that tech companies like to throw around a lot. The two companies in my research were no different, but from what I could tell, when it came to their food programs, they were really following the lead of larger companies like Google that have set expectations in the industry. The value placed on commensality in this context comes from the idea that different departments need to understand what each other department does in order to have a company that can work more cohesively toward goals. This use of commensality, though, has turned a social activity (i.e., eating lunch) into an economic activity, under the guise of sharing ideas and creating community. Doyne Dawson in his book *Cities of Gods: Communist Utopias in Greek Thought* says that in certain parts of ancient Greece, the rich maintained social stability by sharing a water well with the poor (Dawson 1992, 17). This is reminiscent of "rich" companies sharing food with the "poor" employee in order to help create community and cohesion.

The shared food creates a small in-group: those who are able to access the food. In a very physical way, the employees inside the offices are removed from the pee-soaked streets outside. These streets are a daily reminder that the idealization of busyness is taking place in a time and place where many people have no prospects of work at all. James Ferguson (Ferguson 2015) has argued persuasively that social justice requires breaking the link we habitually make between work and the right to a dignified life. He bases this argument largely on his research in South Africa, but I find his insights especially pertinent to the situation in San Francisco. Specifically, he points out that "even in highly proletarianized South Africa . . . broad sectors of the population are largely or wholly excluded from the world of wage labor and instead piece together livelihoods through a complex mix of other activities" (Ferguson 2015, 91). He continues:

> Nor are those who fall outside of the realm of regularized wage labor necessarily peasants or subsistence farmers, either. Instead, as was discussed in the introduction, Africa's fast-growing cities are increasingly inhabited by people who lack both land and formal-sector jobs and who improvise complex and contingent livelihoods through a combination of petty trade, hustling, casual labor, smuggling, prostitution, begging, theft, seeking help from relatives or lovers, and so on. (Ferguson 2015, 91)

Ferguson points out that the Marxist viewpoint and over-valuation of production have led to a cultural valuation of people with neither formal work nor independent wealth as "social refuse, of neither economic or political value—the 'scum, offal and refuse of all classes'" (Ferguson 2015, 91). My experience in these offices in San Francisco hold true to this division—a division of labor, but also a division of morality. Morality for those inside is based on salaried employment; they felt entitled to free food based on their employment, knowing full well that that same entitlement was denied to those on the streets, the group Ferguson calls the "proletariat-in-waiting." The homeless on the street have become such a part of the everyday lives of the employees that they were rarely mentioned during interviews. A notable exception was one employee, mentioned earlier, who was afraid to leave the building. On one occasion, Hannah at Company B told me that she was reluctant to give up her apartment in Oakland because it was rent controlled—even if it was in a "bad part of town"—because she wouldn't be able to afford to live anywhere else. Charlotte at Company A mentioned the cost of living in San Francisco as "extreme." But neither of them talked about the homeless on the streets, the needles, or the smell of urine or commented on many of the terrible aspects about living in San Francisco as reported in various newspaper articles (Fuller 2018).

Is it really any surprise, then, that employees feel entitled? The larger social context reaffirms daily that they are the ones entitled to eat (so long as they continue to work). I believe that donating excess food to homeless shelters and other charities relieves some of the guilt while the entire food program is part of a deep cultural linkage drawn between entitlement and work.

Living on the "crumbs of society" might in itself be a valuable social activity, "along with any recognition that the distributive claims emerging from such forms of life might be either legitimate, or part of a progressive political mobilization" (Ferguson 2015, 92). What I believe is that the tech companies actually need those people on the street to help create and maintain feelings of privilege, gratitude, and happiness for employees who must walk past them every day. It almost works as a reminder: this is what happens to those who don't hustle enough, who don't put in the time required to get things done. It pushes employees to the limits and in some cases, even keeps them in the office because of the smell or fear of the ones who failed.

In the light cast by this intense pressure to work (one's life depends on it!) the traditional lunch hour has less and less appeal. To some employees, lunch is not as important as getting home on time, picking up the kids from school, or getting more sales commission—employees will sacrifice thirty minutes of lunch in exchange for these. Time has value and their time is flexible, so they use that flexibility for their own purposes, instead of the companies'. Many of the employees I talked to mentioned that they understood that free food keeps them at work longer. The surprising thing to me was that most of them admit this, do nothing about it, and realize that they, in turn, give the employer extra hours of work that should be taken as breaks for food and which amount to more value to the company than the food they get for free. For the most part, these extra hours are unpaid. For example, the average contract at Company B in London was forty-five hours a week, with five unpaid lunch hours. As I have said previously, I never once during my time there observed anyone taking a full lunch hour.

Sandra was a sales manager at the London Company A office. She was often the first one to arrive and the last one to leave. She has what can be described as a "good work ethic" or as a "workaholic." She is in her late twenties and lives alone. We talked one day about food and productivity and her insights into her own role and life were revealing:

> Food is not directly linked to my productivity or seeing achievements because in my role as a sales manager, I can see my achievements really easily. I have clear monetary goals that I need to hit. I see the financial rewards of those too through commission payments.

Sandra's sales job is perhaps one of the few that has clear goals and outcomes. In the job description listed online for a sales role, it clearly states: "Exceed monthly/quarterly/annual key performance metrics by selling Company A solutions into new accounts within an assigned vertical market." For team members in communication, marketing, or account management, the goals are less well defined, less "metric" focused. Maria, for example, is responsible for the German accounts and is generally available by phone to help clear up any problems. Yet, her daily goals are not as defined as Sandra's, who only needs to reach a certain number of sales by the end of the week/month/quarter. Maria's jobs are more flexible or agile.

The lunch break has become difficult to categorize as a break. Technology is one reason—checking emails on your phone at lunch is common. Another is that what used to be an opportunity for a private daily interlude has now been ransacked into what companies want to be a community and social event. So, what categorizes a break? For Christopher at Company A in London, a break is just that. He was the only person I encountered in that office who took a full lunch hour each day. He reflected in his interview that in the past, work was less complicated. "You could easily step out, eat at a cafe, read the newspaper, and not have to worry about being contacted by anyone." What would happen if all employees acted as he did? In addition, what about employees who needed space and time in order to generate ideas and be creative?

For employees who feel like they have little control over their lives at work, eating in the office is an opportunity for subversion and rebellion (Bell and Valentine 1997). Christopher was defying the status quo by taking an entire hour. The employee at Company A in San Francisco who brought his own coffee was making a statement against the company's coffee choices. There are small infractions like this all over the place, but the norm is to not bring your own coffee, not take an entire hour for lunch, not cause any issues. The norm is to fall in line.

On Quitting and Layoffs

Neither Kim nor any other of the food program managers were still in their jobs twelve months after my fieldwork. As an office manager for Company A in London, Kim had little room for advancement. She was already a "manager," yet there was no obvious place for her to advance. After working for a couple of years in a role like that, it becomes difficult to see the future. Jennifer had a similar position at Company B in London, as did Hannah at Company B in San Francisco. Perhaps Charlotte at Company A in San Francisco had the most opportunity for advancement in her own office, the global headquarters, yet even she chose to leave for reasons not yet clear to me. Kate, Hannah, Jennifer, and Paolo were all part of the round of layoffs and restructuring that took place at Company B. I tried to stay in touch with all of these people on social media such as LinkedIn, Instagram, and Twitter, but I was unable to do so successfully.

The fact that these employees are not in their roles any longer shows the extent which these people practiced care in a context where there was always the possibility that they could lose their jobs at any minute or choose to leave with barely a glance back. This brings to mind a phrase from Gershon: "Moving on is the new normal." Specifically, she says:

After all, if every job is temporary, and a career is really a string of jobs, then quitting (or getting fired or laid off) is always just around the corner. This is yet another aspect of how the self-as-business metaphor dominates people's strategies in the workplace—a job is now a connection with another business which ideally enables you to enhance your desirability to many other potential employers. Everyone "should" always be anticipating their next job. (Gershon 2017, 207)

Following that she says that quitting is actually a strong critique of the "organization or community that you are no longer willing to be a part of" (Gershon 2017, 207). Were Charlotte and Kim trying to make a statement to the company? Unlikely—what is more likely is that neither of them saw a future with the company.

During my conversation with Martin at Company B, he brought up the fact that if you are an engineer or product manager in Silicon Valley, you're "constantly being pinged by recruiters, and there is just a lot more opportunities, so I think that really leads to people switching jobs more. I think that the average is just over two years at a company." When asked about why people switch jobs, he said, "People move for a lot of reasons—it's very personal. But you know, there's enough opportunity out there that there will be some combination of the project you want to work on, the learning you want to do, the commute you want to have, and then the benefits you want to have." Martin didn't mention food in this equation, probably because it was assumed that there would be food—as I've mentioned before, it's not really an option. But searching for that right combination of things, as he puts it, is key, especially when the salaries are more or less the same across the board for engineers. Looking for a better commute, more interesting project, and training opportunities makes sense.

With that in mind, employees need to have some kind of future, something to look forward to—whether that is advancing in salary and responsibility or title—there must be a clear path forward for them, one that seems achievable. In many tech companies, though, this path is less than clear. Gershon also points out that "by the twenty-first century, pensions were rare and seniority at a company did not go together with a higher salary. Most employees no longer pay any financial penalty for switching jobs" (Gershon 2017, 213).

This connects to what Martin, at Company B, told me: "Many engineers increase their pay without actually ever becoming a manager—which is one of the appeals," he says, "to being an engineer." In other words, your responsibilities can remain pretty much the same and instead of having to deal with the administrative paperwork related to being a manager, you can just get pay increases over time. That is rare in almost any other industry but is supported by evidence from Gershon, who says that "even though moving up within a company is still something to consider, it is no longer people's primary focus" (Gershon 2017, 209). So, is this advancement based on merit, or just time and putting in what those in leadership positions might just call "good behavior" like showing up on time, not being sick too much, and working long hours like everyone else? Can we even call an increase in pay advancement or does advancement need to include a new and more prestigious title? In my view, the entire idea of advancement is outdated and arcane and, in fact, I think that most engineers might agree, at least those who are happy to accept more pay with the same amount of responsibility. Besides, having more middle managers creates situations where bullshit jobs can proliferate (Graeber 2018).

Managers at Company B and Company A do not regulate the workday. For the most part, they are like the Malagasy government that Graeber describes as "not really there" (Graeber 2015, 186). Managers' power ebbs and flows. There are times where they hope that no one will notice that they are managers; they blend in with the use of clothing and the help of the flat office structure. They do not have offices to hide in. Sometimes they might have to make decisions; this seems like something many people I talked to wanted to avoid. But the hierarchy exists, and, in some ways, it has to because that's the way companies are organized. But if your company is slow to grow and you have employees who are eager to move up the ladder, you soon end up with a lot of managers and no subordinates.

Compared to Kim or Charlotte, engineers have bargaining power and skills that are in great demand. They can port their skills around town to different companies without much trouble, showcasing the "product" they worked on before. For those employees without as much bargaining power, free food holds a more prominent place in the office but does not necessarily sway their ideas about where to work. In numerous interviews I conducted, employees told me how they did not take the job for the free food, but because of the people, the company, or other reasons. Food comes into play later when employees consider leaving for a company where free food is not offered. Then, the concept of how much the food matters, how much money and time they save comes to mind. This came up in four different interviews.

> I think it will be a big shock if I took a job somewhere else that didn't have it [free food]. It definitely makes people sit together at lunch a lot more. It definitely brings you all together at lunch, which is a really nice thing. It gets you away from your desk. (Nick, employee, Company A, London)

> I mean, yeah, it would be hard to go back to a place where you just got like, coffee and tea, especially after getting all the snacks like they give you here [at Company B]. (Melanie, employee, Company B, London)

I think [free food] was mentioned in the interview but it wasn't a major theme or anything like that. (Jack, employee, Company A, London)

When they told me that I got free lunch and all the snacks, I took the job immediately. (Katie, employee, Company B, London)

What these extracts show is that eating together and being offered free food make a difference in the work lives of these employees. After Company B's financial issues, which resulted in a cutback of meals and other food perks, there was a sharp decline in the company's ratings on Glassdoor, the career reviews website. As Gelles reports, many of those reviews show a company in decline (Gelles 2017). Company B has not been able to solve its problems with financial stability through the cunning use of taco Tuesday or macaroni and cheese. There was also no indication from the employees that I spoke to that new ideas were ever dreamt up over a sushi station or in the smoothie room. These companies were using food as a crutch and a tool that has helped to create a class of workers reliant on the free meals provided for them. The sense of entitlement to this food is such that they will leave bad reviews, change jobs, or, God forbid, go out for lunch, if the food isn't to their liking.

NOTES

1. See https://www.thriveglobal.com/stories/12750-how-the-creed-of-hustling-is-central-to-silicon-valley-s-workaholism, and https://www.nytimes.com/2017/08/31/opinion/sunday/silicon-valley-work-life-balance-.html.

2. See https://www.theatlantic.com/technology/archive/2018/09/tech-labor-movement/567808/, https://techworkerscoalition.org/, and https://siliconvalleyrising.org/.

Chapter Eight

Conclusion and the Limits of Care

THE BAKE-OFF

"Will you judge the Christmas bake-off for us tomorrow?" Kim asked as I was heading out one day in December. "Sure!" I said, surprised by the unusual request. Kim continued: "Well, last year only two of us . . . made something so don't expect a lot." I thought it kind of humorous that they asked me to judge, but who else if not me, the outsider? I played along wondering why they would continue to do an event that had such little participation.

The next day, I arrived to find that everybody was in good spirits—as if on holiday already, yet there was still a full week to go. Kim put Christmas music on, only to be met with groans from most of the sales team. "It's a bit too early for that, don't you think?"

The bake-off judging happened in the afternoon. There were only four entries, it turned out—a low participation rate. Not exactly what I was expecting, but Kim did warn me that last year there were only two (so there was actually a 100 percent increase in participation). I was presented with dark chocolate muffins with raspberries and a festive frosting; chocolate brownies with walnuts; mince pies; and stollen, a traditional German Christmas cake.

While Kim sat at her desk looking indifferent, typing away at her computer, I tasted and thought about each of the entries—about the work and energy that went into making each dish. I took my time, making notes about the flavor and consistency. The cupcakes were moist and very chocolatey, and the raspberry was a nice touch, but the frosting was too sweet. The brownies were a bit dry, but good nonetheless. The mince pies were excellent—the pastry perfectly crumbly (I presume because it was made with butter) and the filling zesty and sweet. Finally, the stollen was nicely spiced, with a vein of marzipan running down the center and alcohol-soaked raisins dotting each slice . . . it tasted like Christmas.

In the end, the stollen was my pick. Mike, the office director, made the announcement and presented a bottle of champagne to the winner. Then, the entire office descended into the kitchen to taste each of the sweets, make coffee, chitchat, and enjoy the afternoon. By the time I went home that evening there was not a crumb left.

> *Kim:* Thanks for being the judge! I think it went really well.
>
> *Int:* No problem. What did you like the best?
>
> *Kim:* Oh, I didn't try anything, I'm not really eating sugar at the moment.

Kim's response wasn't surprising given her lack of interest in the event. Her body language, her tone of voice—they all registered as tiredness. The bake-off experience was an attempt at caring on my part, but it left me feeling silly for the effort because of the lack of participation and interest.

As I mentioned earlier, at the outset of this research I didn't want to focus on the negative aspects of free food at work and instead, answer the question, how do we understand commensality in the workplace and how does food divide and unite? Yet, as my research progressed, I could not avoid the observation that food programs are often not living up to their full potential in these offices. Some events, like the bake-off, seemed a feeble attempt at caring. Kim was in charge of organizing activities like this, but she never showed much enthusiasm about them—only as much as she needed. This harkens back to the idea mentioned in chapter 6 that employees put in as much work as they need to. This sums up nicely the limits of care within the tech office that was one of my overall observations. Even though she organized the bake-off, Kim didn't care that much about it. She didn't bake anything or even try any of the sweets. Was she just organizing events like this to tick off boxes on her report to her manager (who was actually in San Francisco)? Or was she genuinely trying to get the employees to take part in a collective activity that she passionately believed in? The Christmas party took place later that week (I unfortunately didn't get to attend because of the budget, Kim said) and reportedly had a participation rate of 99 percent. Yet it still appeared to me as if she wasn't invested in the party and what it meant to the employees as opposed to just doing what was expected by others in the office and her manager. There is a difference in the quality of care depending on who the care is really for—the recipient or a performance for someone else?

While I was in the field and writing up, there were a few other food program changes that made the news, also related to care. The most interesting story was that Airbnb decided to stop employing their food workers in-house and made the choice to outsource their food to Bon Appetit—a large catering company that serviced many Silicon Valley companies, including Google. Why was this significant? In-house employees usually have better benefits, perks, and pay—just like any other employee would. Airbnb was one of the few companies left, as I understand it, who had in-house food service workers. It is another example of the limits of care of employees: the food employees, the ones previously employed in the kitchens, had originally been included in the tech industry corporate care but were ultimately excluded from that care. It is another area where we can see a division between service workers and the rest, the kind of division that Paolo, at Company B, wanted to mitigate. The limits of care were also evident in several other instances I observed including the discrepancy between San Francisco offices and the satellite offices in the kind of "care" they got and the discrepancy between the inside of the offices versus the pee-soaked streets. The recurring theme seems to be that care is given to some people but not others, and some are cared for more than others. That is, exclusion is at the heart of this kind of care. No wonder that entitlement was the result: it was implied from the very beginning!

Looking back to the chart in Bock's book that tracks the perks and their associated costs, listed in chapter 2, it's no surprise that the food—and the associated workers—are the first to be downsized, even if they are, as I have shown here, expected. Food programs are expensive. Moving the food production to a catering company saves money in the long run. While it is not surprising economically, it does reveal the nature and limits to the care provided: if this is care, then it is not the limitless care of, say, a mother for her child (although food program managers did have strikingly maternal roles and were likened to mother figures in the office, as per the introduction). It is a qualified, conditional care that can be withdrawn at any time—it is precarious, like their jobs. And it is a care that differentiates workers from one another: some are included in the care, others excluded. Some have the heights of San Francisco pampering; others (such as the in the satellite offices) get greasy reheated deliveries.

At the end of the day, one can't escape the impression that these food programs don't actually make economic sense. What is their purpose, then? As noted by Orwell, a population busy working doesn't have time to do much else—for example, cook or pack a lunch. And one could also say they barely have time to think. Food programs instill on a busy workforce a sense that they are lucky to have the chance to be "in the hustle" at all. Food is a key part of an overall work culture based on valuing being "a hustler" and not "a loser." Food gives these busy workers a sense of privilege and entitlement (instead of a sense of exploitation and outrage at their long working hours and eviscerated private lives). At the same time, it constantly makes clear the limits of care. Workers feel both entitled as members of the in-group but also aware that there is a hierarchy to this in-group, and they need to work hard to climb it or just avoid being excluded altogether. Job loss was an ever-present threat for many of the workers I knew.

What, then, is the limit to this model? The future of tech is now intricately linked to food, at least, until the day in which AI (artificial intelligence) takes over. What then? Will employees be allowed to work in their actual homes? Will companies offer education programs focused on cooking skills and provisioning? Or will new apps and technology replace these needs, too?

THE LIMITS OF CARE

Charlotte, Kim, and Jennifer cared about their jobs, but did it end there? There were moments where I understood that for each of them, part of their job was, as Graeber describes, just box ticking, that is "creating work to show everyone that something is being done" (Graeber 2018, 45).

As I said in the introduction, the sort of care I witnessed in these offices raises the question of whether this is true care at all. Since the care providers are actually paid to do so, one would believe that it is in fact just another type of labor—another job in an office (Lane 2017). Ironically, it's these jobs that are hard to care about. None of the informants who filled these roles told me they were caring for employees; I personally didn't feel particularly cared for either. These roles are an attempt at installing care in an industry where jobs and people are transient and disposable. In the end, the job itself is like many others that require you to send emails, fill out spreadsheets, answer phone calls, and prepare reports.

As my contact with these people grew cold and I realized that I would likely never see any of them again, I felt that the "care" extended in these offices was frail, imposed, false, or even pretend—the kind of care that you get from an airline attendant passing out meals on a long-haul flight, care that has limits of time and energy. As mentioned in chapter 6, all the food program managers were uncontactable six months later. Despite all of the friendly smiles and the conversations that ended in "yes, let's keep in touch," there has been no communication at all from the office managers I worked with. Still, I have come into contact with other tech employees from other companies who showed a real interest in commensality. One day, an employee told me about his first job in a small Yahoo satellite office. There, he and his colleagues would stop each day to gather around a large communal table to eat lunch together. He asked me if this was what "commensality" meant. It is easy to be cynical about institutionalized commensality, but the concept still holds an allure.

Interestingly enough, not long before the holiday season during my field-work, there was an opportunity that I was presented with that, under scrutiny now, perfectly showcases the kind of box ticking and lack of care that I described above.

A Pandemic Arrives and Final Thoughts

This doesn't need much in way of an introduction, but the COVID-19 pandemic of 2020 changed most, if not all, of the office food arrangements discussed here. Employees were shuffled out of offices into their homes. Some, I imagine, were forced to reckon with the idea of provisioning and cooking for themselves for the first time in a while. Some welcomed the change to working from home and many tech companies gave employees substantial top-up-sums for them to purchase equipment for their home office arrangement. Suddenly, basically overnight, the piles of snacks, the buffets of food, the sushi, pizza, burgers, specialty coffee, kombucha, endless LaCroix, and all the rest was gone—suddenly, employees had to buy these things for themselves.

But the pandemic didn't only change what tech employees eat, but it also changed who they eat with, where they eat, and what quality of foods they eat. Eating at home, some with family circles, some with roommates, some with partners, husbands, wives, sisters, brothers. Some alone. The commensality of eating together has definitely been lost. Dining "together" via Zoom is not the same. Gone are also the days of the "casual conversations" and "idea sharing" that was one of the justifications given for free food. It is hard to sit and write about these changes without having spoken to more employees about what that shift looked like. I spoke with a few who reported getting memos from senior management saying that they could not expense food. I talked with others who told me that they eat at their desk at home, oftentimes while still working, and that they miss the opportunity to stand up and walk to a different part of the office for their meal. I spoke with others who were looking for the same thing that many of us were: connection. This lack of connection affected all of us who were shifted into a lockdown situation, not just tech workers.

As things continue to morph and shift, as the pandemic continues to affect us all around the world, tech companies are bringing back a few employees, essential ones, but for the most part employees are going to be at home for a while longer it appears. While a few employees might be treated in the office to snacks, water, coffee (i.e., the basics), others will continue to have to provide for themselves. And while this book has focused on the tech employees themselves, what is not covered here is the immense number of cooks, chefs, dishwashers, baristas, and associated employees within these companies who do the real cooking and cleaning up. What of their jobs? What of their security post-COVID in keeping large numbers of hungry employees fed? There is no one answer, but instead myriad answers and solutions in place around the globe, dependent on not just companies, but countries and governments to step in and help out. What is for sure is that 2020 was a year of great difficulties and while this particular group of employees might seem immune in many ways, their lives have also been affected.

> I walk in and the office music is playing as normal. In the far back of the room, the desks are empty, and the lights are off. All of the account managers are gone today working from home or else on holiday. My last day here was announced but I have not heard from anyone about it. Maybe the office manager forgot to send the email? No one offers to eat lunch with me, and I decide on my own to get a Subway sandwich and bring it back. I sit in the kitchen and eat alone.
>
> It feels slightly emotional being here and I'm very glad now that I'm not going to be spending all of my time in one location, in one office with one group of people. I'm moving on and hope to use what I have discovered here to help me in the other field sites. (Field notes, Company A, London, March 2017)

Not only has the world weathered a pandemic, but there was also the Trump presidency and the United Kingdom vote to leave the European Union. The United Kingdom left, and Trump got impeached, and then the entire world came to a halt. Both Brexit and Trump's success signal an insularity in both countries—coincidentally, an insularity that also plays out in the food programs. The political issues of both countries are a clear example that the division between the haves and have-nots is a real problem. The pee-soaked streets of San Francisco still get hosed down once in a while and city councils are voting to limit new tech offices' ability to provide free meals; however, the problems remain more or less the same, and have maybe even been enhanced by the recent year of pandemic unease. Each time I brought up Brexit in one of the London offices, no one seemed to think it would actually affect them and passed it off as a quirk or something that didn't matter. This is the division between London and the rest of the United Kingdom, which is predominately rural, the haves and have-nots, just in a different context. Maybe what different political sides need to do is share a meal and talk over their differences?

I ate a lot of free meals during my time in the field. What I didn't mention is that many of the meals at Company A were actually eaten alone, including my last one. During those meals, I didn't feel like part of a community; I felt like an outsider who had snuck past the security guard. Company B, as I have highlighted, put a greater focus on commensality and there I always ate with other employees. Company A, while allowing for commensality to happen spontaneously, didn't necessarily encourage it. Some days at Company A it seemed everyone was too busy to stop and eat at the table with me. Some days my introductions at the lunch tables were met with odd looks, inconsequential small talk, or people just ignoring me altogether. Those meals, consumed alone while still surrounded by a lot of people (some also eating alone), were the most isolating, lonely experiences of my fieldwork. In many ways, it shows just how much the standard notion of commensality can be pushed beyond its limits of just eating together at the same table.

The film *Office Space* attests to the absurdist way many employees view office work. This absurdity seems to acknowledge that below the surface are contradictions that, if admitted to, might bring on a crisis. One of these contradictions, I discovered, is that commensality is effective at drawing people together but doesn't change the fact that people might still feel lonely at work. This seems to be the norm: food can't change the fundamental dynamics of the workplace—free food is not enough to make employees happy—free food doesn't always lead to feeling like part of a community.

Commensality could be a secure basis for social relations in organizations where no material objects are being made and where work can be precarious or detached. It is part of being human and offers a kind of stability that these companies don't provide in other areas. It is safe to say that some food programs are not living up to their potential. While these companies continue to innovate—as work practices continue to shift—grounding our lives in the stability of *commensality* will only become more essential.

References

Alvesson, M. 2009. "At-Home Ethnography: Struggling with Closeness and Closure." In *Organizational Ethnography: Studying the Complexities of Everyday Life*, edited by S. Ybema. London: Sage Publications.

Andersen, Sidse S., Lotte Holm, and Charlotte Baarts. 2015. "School Meal Sociality or Lunch Pack Individualism? Using an Intervention Study to Compare the Social Impacts of School Meals and Packed Lunches from Home." *Social Science Information* 54 (3): 394–416. https://doi.org/10.1177/0539018415584697.

Anderson, E. N. 2014. *Everyone Eats: Understanding Food and Culture*. New York: NYU Press.

Appleyard, Bryan. 2021. "Is This the Death of Apple?" *New Statesman*, June 10, 2021. https://www.newstatesman.com/politics/2013/11/death-apple.

Barley, Stephen R., and Pamela S. Tolbert. 1997. "Institutionalization and Structuration: Studying the Links between Action and Institution." *Organization Studies* 18 (1): 93–117. https://doi.org/10.1177/017084069701800106.

Bauccio, Fedele. 2013. "You Are What Your Employees Eat." *Harvard Business Review*, September 24, 2013. https://hbr.org/2013/09/you-are-what-your-employees-eat.

Belasco, W. J., and R. Horowitz. 2009. *Food Chains: From Farmyard to Shopping Cart*. Philadelphia: University of Philadelphia Press.

Bell, D., and G. Valentine. 1997. *Consuming Geographies: We Are Where We Eat*. New York: Routledge.

Benson, P., and S. Kirsch. 2018. "The Capitalist Corporation." In *The International Encyclopedia of Anthropology*, edited by H. Callan. Hoboken, NJ: John Wiley & Sons.

Beriss, D. 2018. "Not Safe Spaces: On Protest & Exclusion in DC Restaurants." *Food Anthropology*. https://foodanthro.com/2018/06/26/not-safe-spaces-on-protest-exclusion-in-dc- restaurants/. Accessed June 27, 2018.

Beriss, D., D. E. Sutton, and I. Ebrary. 2007. *The Restaurants Book: Ethnographies of Where We Eat*. Oxford and New York: Berg.

Bloch, M. 1999. "Commensality and Poisoning." *Social Research* 66 (1): 133–49.

Bock, Laszlo. 2015. *Work Rules! Insights from Inside Google That Will Transform How You Live and Lead.* London: John Murray Publishers.

Bookman, Sonia. 2013. "Coffee Brands, Class and Culture in a Canadian City." *European Journal of Cultural Studies* 16 (4): 405–23. https://doi.org/ 10.1177/1367549413484298.

Bourdieu, Pierre. 1977. *Outline of a Theory of Practice.* Cambridge: Cambridge University Press.

———. (1984) 2015. *Distinction: A Social Critique of the Judgement of Taste.* London and New York: Routledge, Taylor & Francis Group.

Bove, Caron F., Jeffery Sobal, and Barbara S. Rauschenbach. 2003. "Food Choices among Newly Married Couples: Convergence, Conflict, Individualism, and Projects." *Appetite* 40 (1): 25–41. https://doi.org/10.1016/s0195-6663(02)00147-2.

Bowles, N. 2017. "To Fit into Silicon Valley, Wear These Wool Shoes." *The New York Times*, August 11, 2017. https://www.nytimes.com/2018/07/31/technology/ san-francisco-tech-free-lunch.html.

———. 2018. "San Francisco Officials to Tech Workers: Buy Your Lunch." *The New York Times*, July 31, 2018.

Brembeck, Helene. 2005. "Home to McDonald's: Upholding the Family Dinner with the Help of McDonald's." *Food, Culture & Society* 8 (2): 215–26.

Brewis, Joanna, and Christopher Grey. 2008. "The Regulation of Smoking at Work." *Human Relations* 61 (7): 965–87. https://doi.org/10.1177/0018726708093904.

Bronislaw Malinowski. 1954. *Magic Science and Religion and Other Essays.* Garden City, NY: Doubleday.

Brown, Edward. 2017. "The Open Office Plan: How to Gain Collaboration without Losing Concentration." *Nonprofit World* 35 (4): 22–23.

Brown, Linda Keller, and Kay Mussell. 1984. *Ethnic and Regional Foodways in the United States: The Performance of Group Identity.* Knoxville: University of Tennessee Press, Knoxville.

Callan, Hilary. 2018. *The International Encyclopedia of Anthropology.* Hoboken, NJ, and Chichester, West Sussex: Wiley Blackwell.

Cappelli, Peter. 2014. "Google Adds Benefits, Walmart Cuts Them; Oddly, the Logic Is the Same." *Harvard Business Review*, November 7, 2014. https://hbr.org/ 2014/11/google-adds-benefits-walmart-cuts-them-oddly-the-logic-is-the-same.

Caramanica, Jon. 2019. "How to Think about Curiously Fashionable Footwear." *The New York Times*, January 2, 2019, sec. Style. https://www.nytimes.com/2019/01/02/ style/allbirds-birkenstock-stores-new-york.html.

Carrier, James G. 2018. "Gift." In *The International Encyclopedia of Anthropology.* Oxford: John Wiley & Sons.

Chance, Z., R. Dhar, M. Hatzis, and M. Bakker. 2016. "How Google Optimized Healthy Office Snacks." *Harvard Business Review*, April 1, 2016.

Charles, N., and M. Kerr. 1986. "Eating Properly, the Family and State Benefit." *Sociology* 20 (3): 412–29.

Chen, Chao C., Xiao-Ping Chen, and James R. Meindl. 1998. "How Can Cooperation Be Fostered? The Cultural Effects of Individualism-Collectivism." *The Academy of Management Review* 23 (2): 285. https://doi.org/10.2307/259375.

Choi, Mary H. K. 2015. "Letter of Recommendation: LaCroix Sparkling Water." *The New York Times*, March 3, 2015, sec. Magazine. https://www.nytimes.com/2015/03/08/magazine/letter-of-recommendation-lacroix-sparkling-water.html.

Collins, R. 2014. *Interaction Ritual Chains*. Princeton, NJ: Princeton University Press.

Cook, P. H., and A. J. Wyndham. 1953. "Patterns of Eating Behaviour." *Human Relations* 6 (2): 141–60. https://doi.org/10.1177/001872675300600203.

Counihan, Carole. 2004. *Around the Tuscan Table: Food, Family, and Gender in Twentieth Century Florence*. New York: Routledge.

Counihan, Carole, and Penny Van Esterik. 2019. *Food and Culture: A Reader*. New York and London: Routledge.

Cowgill, B., and E. Zitzewitz. 2015. "Corporate Prediction Markets: Evidence from Google, Ford, and Firm X." *The Review of Economic Studies* 82 (4): 1309–41. https://doi.org/10.1093/restud/rdv014.

Cowgill, B., J. Wolfers, and E. Zitzewitz. 2009. "Using Prediction Markets to Track Information Flows: Evidence from Google." In: Das S., Ostrovsky M., Pennock D., Szymanksi B. (eds) Auctions, Market Mechanisms and Their Applications. AMMA 2009. Lecture Notes of the Institute for Computer Sciences, Social Informatics and Telecommunications Engineering, vol 14. Springer, Berlin, Heidelberg. https://doi.org/10.1007/978-3-642-03821-1_2.

Crane, Diana, and Laura Bovone. 2006. "Approaches to Material Culture: The Sociology of Fashion and Clothing." *Poetics* 34 (6): 319–33. https://doi.org/10.1016/j.poetic.2006.10.002.

Crawford, Matthew B. 2015. *The World beyond Your Head: On Becoming an Individual in an Age of Distraction*. New York: Farrar, Straus, and Giroux.

Cunha, Miguel Pina E., Carlos Cabral Cardoso, and Stewart R. Clegg. 2007. "Manna from Heaven: The Exuberance of Food as a Topic for Research in Management and Organization." *SSRN Electronic Journal* 7 (61). https://doi.org/10.2139/ssrn.999645.

D'Costa, Krystal. 2011. "The Culture of Coffee Drinkers." Scientific American Blog Network, August 11, 2011. https://blogs.scientificamerican.com/anthropology-in-practice/the-culture-of-coffee-drinkers/.

———. 2017. "What Do Companies Mean by Culture?" Scientific American Blog Network, August 28, 2017. https://blogs.scientificamerican.com/anthropology-in-practice/what-do-companies-mean-by-culture1/.

Dacin, M. Tina, Kamal Munir, and Paul Tracey. 2010. "Formal Dining at Cambridge Colleges: Linking Ritual Performance and Institutional Maintenance." *Academy of Management Journal* 53 (6): 1393–1418. https://doi.org/10.5465/amj.2010.57318388.

Danesi, Giada. 2017. "A Cross-Cultural Approach to Eating Together: Practices of Commensality among French, German and Spanish Young Adults." *Social Science Information* 57 (1): 99–120. https://doi.org/10.1177/0539018417744680.

Darrah, Charles. 2007. "The Anthropology of Busyness." *Human Organization* 66 (3): 261–69. https://doi.org/10.17730/humo.66.3.n0u0513p464n6046.

Dawson, Doyne. 1992. *Cities of the Gods: Communist Utopias in Greek Thought.* New York: Oxford University Press.

De Botton, Alain. 2008. *The Architecture of Happiness.* New York: Vintage Books.

Chepik, Denis. 2017. "8 Reasons Coffee Improves Office Culture," *Java Republic.* https:// www.javarepublic.com/8-reasons-coffee-improves-office-culture/.

DeVault, M. L. 2013. "Conflict and Deference." In *Food and Culture: A Reader*, edited by C. Counihan and P. Van Esterik, 180–99. New York: Routledge.

Doherty, R. 2017. "The Benefits of an Office Coffee Culture." *Office Coffee Co.* https:// www.office-coffee.co.uk/blog/the-benefits-of-an-office-coffee-culture/.

Douglas, M. 1972. "Deciphering a Meal." *Daedalus* 101 (1): 61–81.

———. 1999. *Implicit Meanings: Selected Essays in Anthropology.* New York and London: Routledge.

Dreyer, Cecily A., and Albert S. Dreyer. 1973. "Family Dinner Time as a Unique Behavior Habitat." *Family Process* 12 (3): 291–301. https://doi.org/10.1111/j.1545 -5300.1973.00291.x.

Elias, Norbert. 1978. *The Civilizing Process.* New York: Urizen Books.

Elsbach, Kimberly D. 2003. "Interpreting Workplace Identities: The Role of Office Décor." *Journal of Organizational Behavior* 25 (1): 99–128. https://doi .org/10.1002/job.233.

English-Lueck, J. A. 2010. *Being and Well-Being: Health and the Working Bodies of Silicon Valley.* Stanford, CA: Stanford University Press.

English-Lueck, J. A., and Miriam Lueck Avery. 2014. "Corporate Care Reimagined: Farms to Firms to Families." In *Epic: Ethnographic Praxis in Industry Conference Proceedings*, 36–49. Oxford: Blackwell Publishing Ltd.

———. 2017. "Intensifying Work and Chasing Innovation: Incorporating Care in Silicon Valley." *Anthropology of Work Review* 38 (1): 40–49. https://doi.org/10.1111/ awr.12111.

Epstein, C. F. 1992. "Tinker-Bells and Pinups: The Construction and Reconstruction of Gender Boundaries at Work." In *Cultivating Differences: Symbolic Boundaries and the Making of Inquality*, edited by M. Lamont and M. Fournier. Chicago: University of Chicago Press.

Feliu, J. 2007. "Nuevas Formas Literarias Para Las Ciencias Sociales: El Caso de la Autoetnografía." *Athenea Digital: Revista de Pensamiento E Investigación Social*, no. 12: 262–71.

Ferguson, James. 2015. *Give a Man a Fish: Reflections on the New Politics of Distribution.* Durham, NC, and London: Duke University Press.

Fischler, C. 1979. "Gastro-nomie et Gastro-anomie." *Communications* 31: 189–210.

———. 1980. "Food Habits, Social Change and the Nature/Culture Dilemma." *Social Science Information* 19 (6): 937–53.

Foster, R. J., and C. Palgrave. 2008. *Coca-Globalization: Following Soft Drinks from New York to New Guinea.* New York: Palgrave Macmillan.

———. 2017. "The Corporation in Anthropology." In *The Corporation: A Critical, Multi-Disciplinary Handbook*, edited by Grietje Baars and Andre Spicer. Cambridge: Cambridge University Press.

Fox, Kate. 2004. *Watching the English: The Hidden Rules of English Behaviour.* London: Hodder & Stoughton.

Fuller, Thomas. 2018. "Life on the Dirtiest Block in San Francisco." *The New York Times*, October 8, 2018, sec. U.S. https://www.nytimes.com/2018/10/08/us/san -francisco-dirtiest-street-london-breed.html.

Gay, Wes. 2016. "How Creating a Culture around Coffee Can Boost Millennial Engagement at Work." *Forbes*, September 16, 2016. https://www.forbes.com/sites/ wesgay/2016/09/16/how-creating-a-culture-around-coffee-can-boost-millennial -engagement-at-work/#73c7585b936a.

Gelles, D. 2017. "Inside the Revolution at Etsy." *The New York Times*, November 25, 2017.

Gershon, Ilana. 2016. "'I'm Not a Businessman, I'm a Business, Man.'" *HAU: Journal of Ethnographic Theory* 6 (3): 223–46. https://doi.org/10.14318/hau6.3.017.

———. 2017. *Down and Out in the New Economy: How People Find (or Don't Find) Work Today*. Chicago and London: The University of Chicago Press.

———. 2018, "Melissa Gregg on Her New Book, *Counterproductive*." *CaMP Anthropology*. https://campanthropology.org/2018/12/17/melissa-gregg-counterproductive/ 2019.

Giles, Jeff. 2019. "What Are You Doing for Lunch?" *The New York Times*, June 21, 2019, sec. Business. https://www.nytimes.com/2019/06/21/business/what-are-you -doing-for-lunch.html.

Given, Lisa M. 2008. *The Sage Encyclopedia of Qualitative Research Methods. Vol. 1*. Los Angeles: Sage Publications.

Gladwell, Malcolm. 2015. *The Tipping Point: How Little Things Can Make a Big Difference*. London: Abacus.

Graeber, David. 2001. *Toward an Anthropological Theory of Value: The False Coin of Our Own Dreams*. New York: Palgrave.

———. 2011. "Consumption." *Current Anthropology* 52 (4): 489–511.

———. 2014a. *Debt: The First 5,000 Years*. Brooklyn, NY: Melville House.

———. 2014b. "On the Moral Grounds of Economic Relations: A Maussian Approach." *Journal of Classical Sociology* 14 (1): 65–77. https://doi.org/ 10.1177/1468795x13494719.

———. 2015. *The Utopia of Rules: On Technology, Stupidity and the Secret Joys of Bureaucracy*. London: Melville House Publishing.

———. 2016. *The Utopia of Rules: On Technology, Stupidity, and the Secret Joys of Bureaucracy*. Brooklyn, NY: Melville House.

———. 2018. *Bullshit Jobs*. New York: Simon & Schuster.

Greenhill, A. 2000. "Reviewed Work: Shoshona Blum-Kulka, *Dinner Talk: Cultural Patterns of Sociability and Socialization in Family Discourse*." *Language in Society* 29 (3): 420–23.

Gregg, M. 2013. *Work's Intimacy*. Oxford: Polity Press.

Griffith, Erin. 2019. "Why Are Young People Pretending to Love Work?" *The New York Times*, January 26, 2019. https://www.nytimes.com/2019/01/26/business/ against-hustle-culture-rise-and-grind-tgim.html.

Gronow, Jukka. 2001. *The Sociology of Taste*. London: Routledge.

Hannerz, Ulf. 2006. "Studying Down, Up, Sideways, Through, Backwards, Forwards, Away, and at Home: Reflections on the Field Worries of an Expansive Discipline." In *Locating the Field: Space, Place and Context in Anthropology*, edited by Simon Coleman and Peter Collins. London: Bloomsbury Academic.

Harvey, David. 1989. *The Condition of Postmodernity: An Enquiry into the Origins of Cultural Change*. Cambridge: Wiley-Blackwell.

Hedge, A. "The Open-Plan Office: A Systematic Investigation of Employee Reactions to Their Work Environment." *Environment and Behavior* 14: 519–42.

High, Holly. 2010. "Ethnographic Exposures: Motivations for Donations in the South of Laos (and Beyond)." *American Ethnologist* 37 (2): 308–22. https://doi.org/10.1111/j.1548-1425.2010.01257.x.

Hirsh, L. 2012. "There Is Some Place like Home: Firm's New Office Space Blends the Best of Both Worlds." *San Diego Business Journal* 33 (23): 17.

Ho, Karen Zouwen. 2009. *Liquidated: An Ethnography of Wall Street*. Durham, NC: Duke University Press.

Hobsbawm, E. J., and T. O. Ranger (eds.). 1984. *The Invention of Tradition*, Past and Present Publications. Cambridge: Cambridge University Press.

Hochschild, Arlie Russell. 1997. *The Time Bind: When Work Becomes Home and Home Becomes Work*. New York: Metropolitan Books.

Horowitz, Alana. 2011. "The One Office Perk You MUST Splurge On." *Business Insider*, March 13, 2011. https://www.businessinsider.com/the-one-office-perk-you-must-splurge-on-2011-3?r=US&IR=T.

Hulst, Merlijn, Sierk Ybema, and D. Yanow. 2017. "Ethnography and Organizational Processes: Studying Processes of Organizing Ethnographically." In *Sage Handbook of Process Organization Studies*, edited by Ann Langley and Tsoukas Haridimos. Los Angeles: Sage Reference.

Isaac, Mike. 2017. "How Uber Deceives the Authorities Worldwide." *The New York Times*, March 3, 2017. https://www.nytimes.com/2017/03/03/technology/uber-greyball-program-evade-authorities.html.

Iyengar, S. 2010. *The Art of Choosing*. New York: Twelve.

Jacoby, Sanford M. 1999. "Are Career Jobs Headed for Extinction?" *California Management Review* 42 (1): 123–45. https://doi.org/10.2307/41166022.

Jennings, Justin, Kathleen L. Antrobus, Sam J. Atencio, Erin Glavich, Rebecca Johnson, German Loffler, and Christine Luu. 2005. "'Drinking Beer in a Blissful Mood.'" *Current Anthropology* 46 (2): 275–303. https://doi.org/10.1086/427119.

Jones, Michael Owen. 2017. "Eating behind Bars: On Punishment, Resistance, Policy, and Applied Folkloristics." *The Journal of American Folklore* 130 (515): 72–108. https://doi.org/10.5406/jamerfolk.130.515.0072.Karr-Wisniewski, Pamela, and Ying Lu. 2010. "When More Is Too Much: Operationalizing Technology Overload and Exploring Its Impact on Knowledge Worker Productivity." *Computers in Human Behavior* 26 (5): 1061–72.

Kaufman, Lindsey. 2014. "Google Got It Wrong. The Open-Office Trend Is Destroying the Workplace." *The Washington Post*, December 30, 2014. https://www.wash

ingtonpost.com/posteverything/wp/2014/12/30/google-got-it-wrong-the-open-of fice-trend-is-destroying-the-workplace/.

Keating, Elizabeth Lillian, and Sirkka L Jarvenpaa. 2016. *Words Matter: Communicating Effectively in the New Global Office*. Oakland: University of California Press.

Kerner, S., C. Chou, and M. Warmind (eds.). 2015. *Commensality: From Everyday Food to Feast*. London: Bloomsbury Academic.

Kniffin, Kevin M., Brian Wansink, Carol M. Devine, and Jeffery Sobal. 2015. "Team Building in the Cafeteria," *Harvard Business Review*, December 2015, 24–25.

Koblin, John. 2015. "Power Lunches Are Out. Crumbs in the Keyboard Are In." *The New York Times*, January 22, 2015, sec. Style. https://www.nytimes.com/2015/01/22/style/power-lunches-are-out-crumbs-in-the-keyboard-are-in.html.

Kohn, Tamara. 2013. "Stuffed Turkey and Pumpkin Pie: In, Through and Out of American Contexts." *Cultural Studies Review* 19 (1). https://doi.org/10.5130/csr.v19i1.3075.

Konnikova, Maria. 2014. "The Open-Office Trap." *The New Yorker*, January 7, 2017. https://www.newyorker.com/business/currency/the-open-office-trap.

La Ganga, Maria L. 2016. "Ordinary People Can't Afford a Home in San Francisco. How Did It Come to This?" *The Guardian*, August 5, 2016. https://www.theguardian.com/business/2016/aug/05/high-house-prices-san-francisco-tech-boom-inequality.

Lamont, M., and M. Fournier. 1995. *Cultivating Differences: Symbolic Boundaries and the Making of Inequality*. Chicago and London: University of Chicago Press.

Lamont, M., S. Pendergrass, and M. Pachucki. 2015. "Symbolic Boundaries." In *International Encyclopedia of the Social and Behavioral Sciences* (2nd edition), edited by J. D. Wright, 850–55. Oxford: Elsevier.

Lanchester, John. 2017. "You Are the Product: It Zucks!" *London Review of Books*, August 17, 2017. https://www.lrb.co.uk/v39/n16/john-lanchester/you-are-the-product.

Lane, Carrie M. 2017. "The Work of Care, Caring at Work: An Introduction." *Anthropology of Work Review* 38 (1): 3–7. https://doi.org/10.1111/awr.12107.

Lee, Wendy, and Roland Li. 2018. "Mountain View's Unusual Rule for Facebook: No Free Food." *San Francisco Chronicle*, July 23, 2018. https://www.sfchronicle.com/business/article/Mountain-View-s-unusual-rule-for-Facebook-No-13096100.php.

Lohr, Steve. 2017. "Don't Get Too Comfortable at That Desk (Published 2017)." *The New York Times*, October 6, 2017, sec. Business. https://www.nytimes.com/2017/10/06/business/the-office-gets-remade-again.html.

Lyons, Dan. 2017. "Opinion: In Silicon Valley, Working 9 to 5 Is for Losers." *The New York Times*, August 31, 2017. https://www.nytimes.com/2017/08/31/opinion/sunday/silicon-valley-work-life-balance-.html.

Malcolm, Hadley. 2015. "Study: The Key to Happiness at Work Is Free Snacks." *USA Today*, September 16, 2015. https://eu.usatoday.com/story/money/2015/09/16/study-says-snacks-affect-happiness-at-work/72259746/.

Malinowski, B. 1948. *Magic, Science, and Religion and Other Essays*. Prospect Heights, NY: Waveland Press.

Marcus, George E. 1995. "Ethnography In/Of the World System: The Emergence of Multi-Sited Ethnography." *Annual Review of Anthropology* 24 (1): 95–117. https://doi.org/10.1146/annurev.an.24.100195.000523.

Marfield, W. 2017. "Don't Even Think about Talking to Me Until I've Had My Second La Croix." *The New Yorker*, September 28, 2017.

Marshall, D. 2005. "Food as Ritual, Routine or Convention." *Consumption Markets & Culture* 8 (1): 69–85.

Martinez, A. G. 2016. *Chaos Monkeys: Mayhem and Mania inside the Silicon Valley Money Machine*. London: Ebury Press.

Mauss, M. 1990. *The Gift: The Form and Reason for Exchange in Archaic Societies*. London and New York: Routledge.

Mauss, Marcel, and W. D. Halls. (1925) 2000. *The Gift: The Form and Reason for Exchange in Archaic Societies*. New York: W. W. Norton.

Merlino, Aldo. 2015. "The Fast and the Furious: Analyzing the Human-Researcher behind the Wheel." *Cultural Studies ↔ Critical Methodologies* 15 (1): 9–14. https://doi.org/10.1177/1532708613516425.

Miller, Daniel. 2013. *Stuff*. Oxford: Wiley.

Mintz, Sidney W. 2013. "Time, Sugar, and Sweetness." In *Food and Culture: A Reader*, edited by C. Counihan and P. Van Esterik. New York: Routledge.

Mohanty, Chandra Talpade. 2007. *Feminism without Borders: Decolonizing Theory, Practicing Solidarity*. Longueuil, Québec: Point Par Point.

Moore, Phoebe V. 2018. "Tracking Affective Labour for Agility in the Quantified Workplace." *Body & Society* 24 (3): 39–67. https://doi.org/10.1177/1357034x18775203.

Morrison, Marlene. 1996. "Sharing Food at Home and School: Perspectives on Commensality." *The Sociological Review* 44 (4): 648–74. https://doi.org/10.1111/j.1467-954x.1996.tb00441.x.

Moussa, Margaret, Mathew Bright, and Maria Estela Varua. 2017. "Investigating Knowledge Workers' Productivity Using Work Design Theory." *International Journal of Productivity and Performance Management* 66 (6). https://doi.org/10.1108/IJPPM-08-2016-0161.

Murcott, A. 1982. "On the Social Significance of the 'Cooked Dinner' in South Wales." *Social Science Information/Information sur Les Sciences Sociales* 21 (4): 677.

Nader, Laura. 1972. *Up the Anthropologist: Perspectives Gained from Studying Up*. ERIC Clearinghouse.

Nast, Condé. 2017. "Don't Even Think about Talking to Me Until I've Had My Second La Croix." *The New Yorker*. September 28, 2017. https://www.newyorker.com/humor/daily-shouts/dont-even-think-about-talking-to-me-until-ive-had-my-second-la-croix.

Nelson, L. 2016. "Why LaCroix Sparkling Water Is Suddenly Everywhere." *Vox*, February 2, 2018.

Ochs, Elinor, Clotilde Pontecorvo, and Alessandra Fasulo. 1996. "Socializing Taste." *Ethnos* 61 (1–2): 7–46. https://doi.org/10.1080/00141844.1996.9981526.

Ochs, Elinor, and Merav Shohet. 2006. "The Cultural Structuring of Mealtime Socialization." *New Directions for Child and Adolescent Development*, no. 111: 35–49. https://doi.org/10.1002/cd.154.

Ortner, Sherry B. 2010. "Access: Reflections on Studying up in Hollywood." *Ethnography* 11 (2): 211–33. https://doi.org/10.1177/1466138110362006.

———. 2016. "Dark Anthropology and Its Others." *HAU: Journal of Ethnographic Theory* 6 (1): 47–73. https://doi.org/10.14318/hau6.1.004. 2017.

Óskarsdóttir, Helga, and Oddsson Guðmundur. 2017. "A Soft Systems Approach to Knowledge Worker Productivity—Analysis of the Problem Situation." Economies 5, no. (3) (2017): 28.

Ostrander, Susan A. 1993. "'Surely You're Not in This Just to Be Helpful.'" *Journal of Contemporary Ethnography* 22 (1): 7–27. https://doi.org/10.1177/089124193022001002.

Palvalin, Miikka, Theo van der Voordt, and Tuuli Jylhä. 2017. "The Impact of Workplaces and Self-Management Practices on the Productivity of Knowledge Workers." *Journal of Facilities Management* 15 (4). https://doi.org/10.1108/JFM-03-2017-0010.

Pao, E. 2018. "Tech Founders' Absolute Power Is Destroying Company Culture." *Wired*, October 10, 2018.

Parker, Martin. 2008. "Eating with the Mafia: Belonging and Violence." *Human Relations* 61 (7): 989–1006. https://doi.org/10.1177/0018726708093905.

Petersen, Anne Helen. 2020. *Can't Even: How Millennials Became the Burnout Generation.* Boston: Houghton Mifflin Harcourt.

Pfeilstetter, R. 2017. "Startup Communities: Notes on the Sociality of Tech-Entrepreneurs in Manchester." *Journal of Comparative Research in Anthropology and Sociology* 8 (1): 1–15.

Prättälä, R., G. Pelto, P. Pelto, M. Ahola, and L. Räsänen. 1993. "Continuity and Change in Meal Patterns: The Case of Urban Finland." *Ecology of Food and Nutrition* 31 (1–2): 87–100.

Robbins, Joel. 2013. "Beyond the Suffering Subject: Toward an Anthropology of the Good." *Journal of the Royal Anthropological Institute* 19 (3): 447–62. https://doi.org/10.1111/1467-9655.12044.

Roseberry, William. 1996. "The Rise of Yuppie Coffees and the Reimagination of Class in the United States." *American Anthropologist* 98 (4): 762–75. https://doi.org/10.1525/aa.1996.98.4.02a00070.

Roy, Donald. 1959. "'Banana Time': Job Satisfaction and Informal Interaction." *Human Organization* 18 (4): 158–68. https://doi.org/10.17730/humo.18.4.07j88hr1p4074605.

Sahlins, Marshall David. 1974. *Stone Age Economics*. London: Tavistock Publications.

Salazar, Melissa L. 2007. "Public Schools, Private Foods: Mexicano Memories of Culture and Conflict in American School Cafeterias." *Food and Foodways* 15 (3–4): 153–81. https://doi.org/10.1080/07409710701620078.

Scheibehenne, Benjamin, Rainer Greifeneder, and Peter M. Todd. 2010. "Can There Ever Be Too Many Options? A Meta-Analytic Review of Choice Overload." *Journal of Consumer Research* 37 (3): 409–25. https://doi.org/10.1086/651235.

Scholliers, Peter. 2001. *Food, Drink and Identity: Cooking, Eating and Drinking in Europe since the Middle Ages*. Oxford: Berg.

Schwartz, B. 2005. *The Paradox of Choice: Why More Is Less*. New York: HarperCollins.

Shankar, Shalini. 2008. *Desi Land: Teen Culture, Class, and Success in Silicon Valley*. Durham, NC: Duke University Press.

Simmel, Georg, David Frisby, and Mike Featherstone. 1997. *Simmel on Culture: Selected Writings*. London and Thousand Oaks, CA: Sage Publications.

Simpson, C. 2015. "How Etsy Eats." *Edible Brooklyn*, November 3, 2015.

Sobal, J., and M. K. Nelson. 2003. "Commensal Eating Patterns: A Community Study." *Appetite* 41 (2) 181–90.

Solon, O. 2017. "Scraping By on Six Figures? Tech Workers Feel Poor in Silicon Valley's Wealth Bubble." *The Guardian*, February 27, 2017.

Stein, Felix. 2017. *Work, Sleep, Repeat: The Abstract Labour of German Management Consultants*. London and New York: Bloomsbury Academic.

Strangleman, Tim. 2010. "Food, Drink and the Cultures of Work." *Food, Culture & Society* 13 (2): 257–78. https://doi.org/10.2752/175174410x12633934463231.

Streitfeld, D. 2018. "Welcome to Zucktown. Where Everything Is Just Zucky." *The New York Times*, March 21, 2018.

Surowiecki, James. 2014. "The Cult of Overwork." *The New Yorker*. January 19, 2014. https://www.newyorker.com/magazine/2014/01/27/the-cult-of-overwork.

Sutton, David E. 2004. "Ritual, Continuity and Change: Greek Reflections." *History and Anthropology* 15 (2): 91–105. https://doi.org/10.1080/0275720041000168993 6.

Swisher, K. 2018. "The Politicians Are Coming for Silicon Valley." *The New York Times*, September 4, 2018.

Thaler, R. H., and C. R. Sunstein. 2009. *Nudge: Improving Decisions about Health, Wealth, and Happiness*. London: Penguin.

Thring, O. 2011. "The Restaurant 'Family' Meal." *The Guardian*, September 5, 2011.

Trubek, Amy B. 2017. *Making Modern Meals: How Americans Cook Today*. Oakland: University of California Press.

Warde, Alan. 1997. *Consumption, Food, and Taste: Culinary Antinomies and Commodity Culture*. London and Thousand Oaks, CA: Sage Publications.

Watson, James. 2016. "Feeding the Revolution: Public Mess Halls and Coercive Commensality in Maoist China." The Handbook of Food and Anthropology. By Jakob A. Klein, James L. Watson, 308–20. London: Bloomsbury Academic. Bloomsbury Food Library. http://dx.doi.org/10.5040/9781474298407.0023.

Weiner, A. B. 1977. *Women of Value, Men of Renown: New Perspectives in Trobriand Exchange*. St. Lucia: University of Queensland Press.

West, Paige. 2012. *From Modern Production to Imagined Primitive: The Social World of Coffee from Papua New Guinea*. Durham, NC: Duke University Press.

Wilk, Richard. 2010. "Power at the Table: Food Fights and Happy Meals." *Cultural Studies: Critical Methodologies* 10 (6): 428–36. https://doi.org/10.1177/1532708610372764.

———. 2015. "Paradoxes of Jews and Their Foods." In *Jews and Their Foodways*, edited by A. Helman. Oxford: Oxford University Press.